Christopher Isherwood

Titles in the series Critical Lives present the work of leading cultural figures of the modern period. Each book explores the life of the artist, writer, philosopher or architect in question and relates it to their major works.

In the same series

Hannah Arendt *Samantha Rose Hill*
Antonin Artaud *David A. Shafer*
John Ashbery *Jess Cotton*
Roland Barthes *Andy Stafford*
Georges Bataille *Stuart Kendall*
Charles Baudelaire *Rosemary Lloyd*
Simone de Beauvoir *Ursula Tidd*
Samuel Beckett *Andrew Gibson*
Walter Benjamin *Esther Leslie*
John Berger *Andy Merrifield*
Leonard Bernstein *Paul R. Laird*
Joseph Beuys *Claudia Mesch*
Jorge Luis Borges *Jason Wilson*
Constantin Brancusi *Sanda Miller*
Bertolt Brecht *Philip Glahn*
Charles Bukowski *David Stephen Calonne*
Mikhail Bulgakov *J.A.E. Curtis*
William S. Burroughs *Phil Baker*
Byron *David Ellis*
John Cage *Rob Haskins*
Albert Camus *Edward J. Hughes*
Fidel Castro *Nick Caistor*
Paul Cézanne *Jon Kear*
Coco Chanel *Linda Simon*
Noam Chomsky *Wolfgang B. Sperlich*
Jean Cocteau *James S. Williams*
Joseph Conrad *Robert Hampson*
H.D. (Hilda Doolittle) *Lara Vetter*
Salvador Dalí *Mary Ann Caws*
Charles Darwin *J. David Archibald*
Guy Debord *Andy Merrifield*
Claude Debussy *David J. Code*
Gilles Deleuze *Frida Beckman*
Fyodor Dostoevsky *Robert Bird*
Marcel Duchamp *Caroline Cros*
Sergei Eisenstein *Mike O'Mahony*
Frantz Fanon *James S. Williams*
William Faulkner *Kirk Curnutt*
Gustave Flaubert *Anne Green*
Ford Madox Ford *Max Saunders*
Michel Foucault *David Macey*
Benjamin Franklin *Kevin J. Hayes*
Sigmund Freud *Matthew ffytche*
Mahatma Gandhi *Douglas Allen*
Antoni Gaudí *Michael Eaude*
Jean Genet *Stephen Barber*
Allen Ginsberg *Steve Finbow*
Johann Wolfgang von Goethe *Jeremy Adler*
Günter Grass *Julian Preece*
Ernest Hemingway *Verna Kale*
Langston Hughes *W. Jason Miller*
Victor Hugo *Bradley Stephens*
Zora Neale Hurston *Cheryl R. Hopson*
Aldous Huxley *Jake Poller*
J.-K. Huysmans *Ruth Antosh*
Christopher Isherwood *Jake Poller*
Derek Jarman *Michael Charlesworth*
Alfred Jarry *Jill Fell*
James Joyce *Andrew Gibson*
Carl Jung *Paul Bishop*
Franz Kafka *Sander L. Gilman*

Frida Kahlo *Gannit Ankori*
Søren Kierkegaard *Alastair Hannay*
Yves Klein *Nuit Banai*
Arthur Koestler *Edward Saunders*
Akira Kurosawa *Peter Wild*
D. H. Lawrence *David Ellis*
Lenin *Lars T. Lih*
Jack London *Kenneth K. Brandt*
Pierre Loti *Richard M. Berrong*
Rosa Luxemburg *Dana Mills*
Jean-François Lyotard *Kiff Bamford*
René Magritte *Patricia Allmer*
Gustav Mahler *Stephen Downes*
Stéphane Mallarmé *Roger Pearson*
Thomas Mann *Herbert Lehnert and Eva Wessell*
Gabriel García Márquez *Stephen M. Hart*
Karl Marx *Paul Thomas*
Henri Matisse *Kathryn Brown*
Guy de Maupassant *Christopher Lloyd*
Herman Melville *Kevin J. Hayes*
Henry Miller *David Stephen Calonne*
Yukio Mishima *Damian Flanagan*
Eadweard Muybridge *Marta Braun*
Vladimir Nabokov *Barbara Wyllie*
Pablo Neruda *Dominic Moran*
Friedrich Nietzsche *Ritchie Robertson*
Georgia O'Keeffe *Nancy J. Scott*
Richard Owen *Patrick Armstrong*
Octavio Paz *Nick Caistor*
Fernando Pessoa *Bartholomew Ryan*
Pablo Picasso *Mary Ann Caws*
Edgar Allan Poe *Kevin J. Hayes*
Ezra Pound *Alec Marsh*
Sergei Prokofiev *Christina Guillaumier*
Marcel Proust *Adam Watt*
Sergei Rachmaninoff *Rebecca Mitchell*
Arthur Rimbaud *Seth Whidden*
John Ruskin *Andrew Ballantyne*
Jean-Paul Sartre *Andrew Leak*
Erik Satie *Mary E. Davis*
Arnold Schoenberg *Mark Berry*
Arthur Schopenhauer *Peter B. Lewis*
Dmitry Shostakovich *Pauline Fairclough*
Adam Smith *Jonathan Conlin*
Susan Sontag *Jerome Boyd Maunsell*
Gertrude Stein *Lucy Daniel*
Stendhal *Francesco Manzini*
Igor Stravinsky *Jonathan Cross*
Rabindranath Tagore *Bashabi Fraser*
Pyotr Tchaikovsky *Philip Ross Bullock*
Dylan Thomas *John Goodby and Chris Wigginton*
Leo Tolstoy *Andrei Zorin*
Leon Trotsky *Paul Le Blanc*
Mark Twain *Kevin J. Hayes*
Richard Wagner *Raymond Furness*
Alfred Russel Wallace *Patrick Armstrong*
Simone Weil *Palle Yourgrau*
Tennessee Williams *Paul Ibell*
Ludwig Wittgenstein *Edward Kanterian*
Virginia Woolf *Ira Nadel*
Frank Lloyd Wright *Robert McCarter*

Christopher Isherwood

Jake Poller

REAKTION BOOKS

For Ayako

Published by Reaktion Books Ltd
Unit 32, Waterside
44–48, Wharf Road
London N1 7UX, UK
www.reaktionbooks.co.uk

First published 2025
Copyright © Jake Poller 2025

All rights reserved

No part of this publication may be reproduced, stored in a retrieval system, or transmitted, in any form or by any means, electronic, mechanical, photocopying, recording or otherwise, without the prior permission of the publishers

Printed and bound in Great Britain by Bell & Bain, Glasgow

A catalogue record for this book is available from the British Library

ISBN 978 1 83639 009 1

Contents

Abbreviations 7
Introduction: Autofiction 9
1 The Poshocracy, 1904–25 16
2 Tea-Tabling, 1925–30 28
3 The Lost, 1931–7 49
4 Ivar Avenue, 1938–44 71
5 *Samsara*, 1945–53 100
6 Kitty and Dobbin, 1954–64 122
7 Life Writing, 1965–80 148 140
Epilogue 169

References 179
Select Bibliography 192
Acknowledgements 196
Photo Acknowledgements 197

Isherwood, *c.* 1940.

Introduction: Autofiction

The work of Christopher Isherwood has proved hard to categorize. His first two novels – *All the Conspirators* (1928) and *The Memorial* (1932) – exhibit many of the hallmarks of modernism, such as interior monologues, and bear the influence of James Joyce and Virginia Woolf. In the 1930s, Isherwood was identified with the Auden Group, which included W. H. Auden, Stephen Spender, Edward Upward, Cecil Day-Lewis and Louis MacNeice, who were ostensibly unified through their anti-fascist stance, their age and their Oxbridge education. George Orwell affirmed that the Auden Group dominated the landscape of British literature in the mid- to-late 1930s as surely as James Joyce and T. S. Eliot had done in the previous decade.[1] Isherwood's style at this time was considered realist, rather than modernist, consistent with his narrator's claim in *Goodbye to Berlin* (1939): 'I am a camera with its shutter open, quite passive, recording, not thinking' (*GB*, 7).

After Isherwood emigrated to the United States in 1939, critics bifurcated his work into English and American phases. The English Isherwood was feted for the novels *Mr Norris Changes Trains* (1935) and *Goodbye to Berlin*, which documented the lives of working-class Germans and bohemian expatriates during Hitler's rise to power through the disinterested 'camera eye' of a narrator resembling Christopher Isherwood.[2] In contrast, the American Isherwood was regarded by British critics as a coward for fleeing from the Second World War. Isherwood had become a pacifist and was studying to be a Hindu monk with the Vedanta Society of Southern California, and he was pilloried for mystic navel-gazing while his fellow countrymen fought against the Nazis. While Isherwood ultimately left the Hollywood Vedanta Center and chose to resume his career as a writer, he continued to work with his guru, Swami Prabhavananda, on translations of key Hindu texts. The novels that he produced while living in America attempted to reflect his spiritual interests and were largely vilified by British critics, who lamented the demise of the politically engaged English Isherwood. In the twenty-first century, American critics, such as James Berg and Chris Freeman, have valorized the American Isherwood, arguing that *A Single Man* (1964) is his masterpiece.[3]

Although astute readers were aware that many of Isherwood's characters were queer, including his namesake narrator in *Goodbye to Berlin*, *Prater Violet* (1945) and *Down There on a Visit* (1962), it wasn't until the publication of his family memoir *Kathleen and Frank* (1971) that Isherwood referred to himself as a homosexual in print. He'd long felt slightly sheepish about dissembling the sexuality of Herr Issyvoo in *Goodbye to Berlin*, but had justified it on aesthetic grounds to the college students he taught in the 1960s by arguing that to make him openly homosexual would have arrogated too much attention to his narrator, who was meant to be a passive camera recording the dramas of Sally Bowles, Otto Nowak and Frl. Schroeder.[4] Emboldened by the gay liberation movement, Isherwood wrote candidly about his sex life in Berlin in the autobiography *Christopher and His Kind* (1976), and made a point of identifying himself as homosexual in interviews.[5] But while he was happy to be an icon for the gay liberation movement, he found the category of gay writing problematic, and advised Armistead Maupin not to allow *Tales of the City* (1978) to be labelled a gay book.[6] Conversely, Isherwood's work has been considered problematic by certain queer theorists, partly because he used the word 'queer' to denote gay men, which goes against the grain of contemporary conceptions of sexuality as a spectrum rather than a binary opposition of heterosexual and homosexual.[7]

In the 1990s, Isherwood's work began to be identified with another category: autofiction.[8] The term is associated with the

French author Serge Doubrovsky, who described his novel *Fils* (1977) as: 'Fiction, of strictly real events and facts; *autofiction* if you like'.[9] The definition of autofiction has been vigorously contested, and I cannot do justice to the debate here. Put simply, it's a genre in which the boundaries between autobiography and fiction are knowingly elided by the author. While some critics have argued that autofiction denotes books classified as fiction in which the protagonist or narrator shares the same name as the author – for example, *I Love Dick* (1997) by Chris Kraus or *My Struggle* (2009–11) by Karl Ove Knausgård – nowadays the term can also be applied to texts classified as autobiographies that deploy fictional structures and techniques, such as the use of scenes and dialogue, and that interrogate the permeability of fact and fiction.[10] Despite being a relatively recent genre, autofiction can be retrospectively applied to works from the past, such as Goethe's autobiography *Poetry and Truth* (1848).[11]

The category of autofiction, then, can be usefully applied both to Isherwood's novels with a namesake narrator and his autobiographies. *Goodbye to Berlin*, *Prater Violet* and *Down There on a Visit* are all narrated by 'Christopher Isherwood', are largely derived from the 'real events' of his life, and include diary extracts (some real and some fictional). In his first autobiography, *Lions and Shadows* (1938), Isherwood instructs the reader to regard the book as fiction, since he has used *noms de guerre* for his friends and employed a 'novelist's licence' to dramatize the material. Furthermore, his publisher (the Hogarth Press) issued the book as a fiction.[12] In *Christopher and His Kind*, however, Isherwood asserts that unlike *Lions and Shadows* his new autobiography will be 'frank and factual' (*CK*, 1). Despite this assertion, he employs *noms de guerre*, structures the book like a novel and includes a suspicious amount of dialogue some four decades after the event. In addition, the book exhibits an autofictive fascination with the distortions that fiction imposes on fact. For example, Isherwood quotes a captious letter from Stephen Spender, who, after reading *Goodbye to Berlin*, complained that Isherwood's character Natalia Landauer was a caricature of her inspiration, Gisa Soloweitschik. To make amends, in *Christopher and His Kind*,

Isherwood attempts to disentangle the real Gisa from the fictional Natalia, but as Spender pointed out in his review of the book Isherwood's factual portrait of Gisa Soloweitschik is just as fictional as his portrait of Natalia Landauer, since ultimately they are both his representations.[13]

Even Isherwood's diaries can be interpreted as autofiction. In *Christopher and His Kind*, Isherwood quotes the following extract from his diary, written on the eve of his departure from Nazi Germany in May 1933:

> And now the day which seemed too good, too bad to be true, the day when I should leave Germany, has arrived, and I only know about the Future that, however often and however variously I have imagined it to myself, the reality will be quite quite different. (*CK*, 138)

In fact, Isherwood confides, he never imagined the day he should leave Germany, and maintains that he only wrote the diary entry because he felt he had to write something solemn and magniloquent to commemorate the historic moment. In this manner, Isherwood would fictionalize his diaries. Furthermore, when he lent the writer Dodie Smith his diaries from 1939 to 1944 (a period when they both lived in Los Angeles), she was scandalized that he had 'faked several journal entries' concerning herself, borrowing details and impressions from a later date and retrospectively applying them to her.[14] Similarly, in a diary entry from 1955, Isherwood affirmed that the heterosexual Tony Duquette 'wants to get to know me better because he sees me as representing the opposite of the chichi life he has to lead as a decorator', and then added: 'This isn't true, but that makes no difference' (*D1*, 493). It seems highly likely that he recorded in his diary other observations he knew to be false – or in other words, that he knew to be fictional – but neglected to mention that they weren't true.

There was also the fact that from the age of six, when Isherwood and his mother collaborated on his first book, *The History of My Friends*, he had been spinning an elaborate mythos about himself.

When his father died in the First World War, Isherwood rebelled at the role he was expected to play – the dutiful son of the 'hero-father', who would be extra pious, work extra hard and uncritically swallow all the patriotic cant spouted by schoolmasters, clergymen and politicians. In response, he made his father into the 'anti-heroic hero' by magnifying certain aspects of his personality – his artistic skill, his contempt for military convention, his fondness for poetry and knitting – and by downplaying his father's military career (at the time of his death, Frank Isherwood was a lieutenant colonel in the army who commanded a battalion of the York and Lancaster Regiment). In contrast, Isherwood's mother Kathleen excelled in her role as 'holy widow', whose incommunicable grief isolated her from her eldest son, and consequently Isherwood cast her in another role, the 'demon-mother'. Whatever his demon-mother loved – such as the past and that arch-emblem of the past, Marple Hall, the Isherwood family seat – he condemned. So dominant was the demon-mother archetype in Isherwood's imagination that it affected his portrayal of mothers in his early fiction and his treatment of Kathleen in real life, resulting in her omission from *Lions and Shadows* (notwithstanding a derisive reference to his 'female relative').

Out of all the categories, then, advanced thus far for Isherwood's oeuvre, autofiction is the most pertinent. Admittedly, not all of Isherwood's work can be regarded as autofiction, such as the novels in which the autobiographical character bears another name, but a substantial portion of his oeuvre, and I would argue the *best* of his oeuvre – *Lions and Shadows*, *Goodbye to Berlin*, *Prater Violet*, *Down There on a Visit*, *Christopher and His Kind* as well as the *Diaries* (1996–2012) – can be fruitfully read as autofiction.[15] In an essay from 1995, Edmund White claimed that 'the characteristic form of gay fiction in the 20th century, from Proust to Genet to Isherwood, is "autofiction",' which combines 'two very different literary traditions, realism and the confession.'[16] Realism, White argued, is essentially secular and emerged in the eighteenth century in opposition to religious art and literature, while the confession is inescapably religious. And these two strands are clearly legible in

Isherwood's work. According to White, queer writers adopted autofiction because it confers

> both the prestige of confession (this is my story, only I have the right to tell it, and no one can challenge my authority in this domain), and the total freedom of imaginative invention (I'm a novelist, I can say whatever I please, and you can't hold me responsible for the opinions expressed by my characters, not even by my narrator).[17]

This last aspect is exemplified by Isherwood in his preface to *Goodbye to Berlin*, in which he instructs the reader not to presume that the book is 'purely autobiographical' just because he and his narrator share the same name.

So far, there have been four biographies of Isherwood. Both *Isherwood: A Biography of Christopher Isherwood* (1977) by Jonathan Fryer and *Christopher Isherwood: A Critical Biography* (1979) by Brian Finney were published prior to Isherwood's death in 1986 and do not benefit from the later scholarly apparatus, such as the *Diaries* and the new criticism that has been published in the twenty-first century. Isherwood judged Fryer's book 'hopelessly dull' and complained that the author had failed to evoke his character; he 'just goes on and on, doggedly listing events, and missing the *point* of them' (*D*3, 533). He was equally dismissive of 'Finney's wretched book' (*D*3, 561), though I would argue that it is far superior to Fryer's biography, and his criticism of Isherwood's work is consistently insightful. Peter Parker's *Isherwood: A Life* (2004) is an impressive and scholarly biography, but it is almost 1,000 pages long and is much more focused on Isherwood's life than his work. Much the same can be said for Katherine Bucknell's *Christopher Isherwood Inside Out* (2024). Bucknell has worked closely with the Isherwood estate for thirty years, exhaustively edited his diaries and letters and has produced the authorized biography. The works of both Parker and Bucknell have been an invaluable resource.

In contrast to conventional biographies, I have attempted to apportion equal space to the life and the work. Given the concise nature of the Critical Lives series, my canvas has been too small to include more than a handful of Isherwood's myriad friends and lovers. Regrettably, even famous friends, such as Igor Stravinsky and Truman Capote, have not made the cut. For similar reasons, I have excluded Isherwood's short stories, the plays he wrote with Auden and the TV and film collaborations with his partner Don Bachardy. Likewise, Isherwood's Hollywood career and his very extensive travels have been given an abbreviated treatment. But the wistful omission of the above has made possible a more expansive analysis of Isherwood's work, and it is my hope that readers of this biography will seek out his less vaunted books – *The Memorial, Lions and Shadows, Prater Violet, My Guru and His Disciple* (1980) and all three volumes of the *Diaries*.

1
The Poshocracy, 1904–25

As an adult, Isherwood often railed against his class: the landed gentry were part and parcel of the motley establishment enemies he dramatically dubbed 'the combine' as an undergraduate at the University of Cambridge. His best friend Edward Upward had coined the pejorative term 'poshocracy' to describe the social elite of Cambridge, who hailed from the best families and schools, derided highbrows and were good at football and cricket. But Isherwood's animosity towards the combine and the poshocracy had nothing to do with the pseudo-communist stance he affected in the 1930s. Even at Cambridge he was very much at home among the members of his class, and secretly enjoyed the company of the poshocracy – he would pretend to Upward that he was a double agent spying on the enemy. And as far as the poshocracy was concerned, Isherwood was 'quite presentable'; he didn't have 'pimples or a grammar-school accent'; and discreet enquiries had revealed that he came from a 'county family' with a decent pile in Cheshire (*LS*, 37).

The Isherwood pile, Marple Hall, was located southeast of Stockport, on the periphery of the Peak District. It was an imposing Elizabethan mansion that had suffered new architectural wrinkles in the nineteenth century, such as the Victorian bay windows at the back of the house, the addition of a squat portico and a Gothic conservatory. Inside, it possessed the traditional trappings of a country seat, including coats of arms, ancestral portraits, stags' heads, oak panelling, Flemish tapestries and suits of armour. The Bradshaw Room included an especially regal four-poster bed; this is where Isherwood's most infamous ancestor, 'Bradshawe the

Regicide', reputedly slept. John Bradshaw (1602–1659) was a staunch republican and friend of John Milton who presided over the trial of Charles I.[1] In the seventeenth century fond royalists held that the king ruled by divine right, and Charles refused to acknowledge the secular authority of the high court of justice by pleading innocent or guilty. It was only after Bradshaw, as lord president, had handed down the death sentence that Charles petitioned the court to speak, but Bradshaw refused to hear him.

In 1606 John Bradshaw's grandfather had purchased Marple Hall, as well as the more modest Wyberslegh Hall, and some twenty farms that comprised the estate. All was well with the Bradshaw line until the eighteenth century, when, in the absence of a male heir, the estate passed to Mary Bradshaw and her second husband, Nathaniel Isherwood, a felt manufacturer from Lancashire who was regarded by the Bradshaws as a parvenu. Thereafter, the family flirted with the double-barrelled surname Bradshaw-Isherwood, but this seems to have been adopted or not at whim; Christopher Isherwood's pretentious Uncle Henry preferred the hyphenated version while his father Frank felt it was an affectation. As the eldest of three sons, Henry was the heir to Marple Hall and could afford to devote his time to drinking at his club, hobnobbing with Italian contessas, and sexual encounters with dashing guardsmen and

Marple Hall, 1898.

biddable proles; Frank (the second son) had to work for a living, and after being educated at Cambridge and Sandhurst, he became an army officer. But Frank was not a typical military man: he was interested in poetry and art, played the piano and enjoyed performing female roles in amateur dramatics.

Isherwood's mother, Kathleen Machell Smith, came from an upper-middle-class family. Her father was a wine merchant from Bury St Edmunds, while her mother came from the Greene family, who had made their money in brewing. Kathleen's uncle, Sir Walter Greene, was a Conservative MP and a Justice of the Peace, and received a baronetcy in 1900. The Greenes might have had a hereditary title but snobbish Uncle Henry regarded them as nouveau riche, since their money derived from commerce rather than the real aristocratic business of owning land. Kathleen first met Frank in the summer of 1895 – he was 26, a wiry lieutenant in the York and Lancaster Regiment with a trim military moustache – and over the next few years they discovered shared interests in painting, architecture and the theatre. Their engagement was beset by punctilious objections from her father and interrupted by Frank's participation in the Boer War, and it wasn't until 17 March 1903 that they were finally married.

Frank's father had agreed to renovate Wyberslegh Hall for the newlyweds. Wyberslegh was a smaller, less ostentatious house than Marple, some 3 miles away near the village of High Lane. It included a farm at the back, with cowsheds and barns, which was let to tenants; Kathleen and Frank occupied the front of the house, which had been built in the fifteenth century. And it was in Wyberslegh that their eldest son, Christopher William Bradshaw Isherwood, was born on 26 August 1904.

As soon as Isherwood was born, Kathleen began to document and mythologize his life. First, in *The Baby's Progress*, a handmade book which she adoringly illustrated and designed, featuring sketches of Wyberslegh and Christopher. In 1906 she began a history of the Bradshaw-Isherwood family (Kathleen reverently used the hyphen), which included a history of Marple and Wyberslegh Halls illustrated with her watercolours and sketches, a potted biography of Bradshaw the Regicide and several family trees. A few years later, Kathleen and Christopher began *The History of My Friends*, which strikes a comically precocious tone: 'I first met Arthur Forbes in December 1909 when we returned from Frimley to Marple. He was just going to be four. He made up all sorts of wonderful things that he meant to do when he was five, just as if five was when you were grown up' (*KF*, 353). A later entry, when Isherwood was about eight, reads: 'I first met Eddie at the drill class last year. It was then our great friendship began.' Eddie evidently usurped a boy named Jack, 'who had long been cool [and] presently I told him I had entirely cast him off, that his chances were gone and I was now best friends with Eddie. I think this annoyed him' (*KF*, 385). Some of his finest work – *Lions and Shadows*, *Goodbye to Berlin*, *Down There on a Visit*, *Christopher and His Kind* – could be described as an artful history of his friends, and all his books elaborated the Christopher Isherwood mythos.

It was common for boys of Isherwood's era and class to be devoted to their nannies, who did the repetitive chores of child-rearing and spent much more time with their charges than either of the parents. Isherwood affirmed that it wasn't until he was almost five that his mother first helped him bathe and dress. In her defence, he noted that both Frank and Kathleen's mother Emily made great demands on her time and attention. In *Kathleen and Frank*, he describes Emily as a 'psychosomatic virtuoso who could produce high fevers, large swellings and mysterious rashes within the hour' when she wasn't getting her way, or when her husband Frederick or Kathleen were insufficiently sedulous in their attentions (*KF*, 11). After Frederick's death in 1905, Emily became particularly needy and deployed a variety of improbable ailments such as throat gout that required Kathleen to drop everything and care for her in London.

At the start of 1912 the Isherwoods moved to Limerick in Ireland, where Frank's regiment was stationed. Kathleen (now in her early forties) had given birth to another son, Richard, the previous year. She sent Christopher to Miss Mercer's High School for Girls, where he was one of the only boys. Kathleen often lamented Christopher's passivity and inability to retaliate against insults, especially from a beguiling bad girl named Mirabel whom he followed 'like a dog, even though she hits him and makes him cry' (*KF*, 379). Consequently, Kathleen decided to send Christopher to a boys' school in the hope that male company would make him more conventionally masculine. Somewhat surprisingly, Isherwood speculated that if he'd been kept at a co-educational school in his teens, he might even have become a heterosexual and expressed relief that he'd been sent to same-sex boarding schools. 'Despite the humiliations', he writes, 'of living under a heterosexual dictatorship and the fury he has often felt against it, Christopher has never regretted being as he is. He is now quite certain that heterosexuality wouldn't have suited him; it would have fatally cramped his style' (*KF*, 384).[2]

The following year Isherwood was sent to St Edmund's, a preparatory school in Hindhead, Surrey, where he was a popular pupil. His teachers reported that he was highly intelligent, with a natural aptitude for English, but was too indolent to apply himself, particularly in the subjects he disliked. He was oppressed by the crushing heterosexual seriousness of team sports, but got an erotic kick out of wrestling and boxing. Indeed, he would later write: 'At St. Edmund's, all of his orgasms with other boys had been while wrestling' (*LY*, 57).

The Isherwoods' time in Limerick came to an end with the outbreak of the First World War. Frank's regiment was mobilized on 4 August 1914, and they were at the front in September. The enforced propinquity of trench life soon began to grate: 'I am afraid I am not a Christian,' he wrote to Kathleen, 'at least perhaps I am. I don't find it at all difficult to love my enemy – but one's friends! Sometimes one feels one can't bear the sight of them' (*KF*, 427).

Frank was given command of the 1st Battalion, who were stationed at Ypres in April 1915. He attempted to reassure Kathleen that 'the worst of the fighting is over' (*KF*, 457). But on 8 May the 1st Battalion was ordered to launch a foredoomed counter-attack on the German front line at Frezenberg, and it seems likely that it was in this offensive that Frank was killed (though the exact circumstances of his death were never confirmed). There began an excruciating period of uncertainty for Kathleen. At first, she was informed by the War Office that Frank was wounded, but there was no trace of him in any of the hospitals, either in England or France. Kathleen received contradictory reports from various contacts: it was Frank's arm that had been injured; his leg had been hit by a piece of shrapnel; one soldier maintained that he was taken prisoner while another reported that Frank was killed by his side while leading an attack on German trenches. Still another report had it that Frank was killed by a shell while being driven to hospital in an ambulance. Finally, on 24 June she was notified by the Red Cross that Frank's dog-tags had been found on a dead soldier near Frezenberg in early May. Kathleen wrote in her diary that 'there appeared a vista of endless hopeless days of loneliness ahead,' in which all her happy memories of Frank had been transformed into 'stabs of pain' (*KF*, 472).

In the Isherwood mythos, Frank's death ossified Kathleen's cult of the past – with their time at Wyberslegh Hall representing a paradise lost – and galvanized Isherwood's rejection of it. At St Edmund's, he was allowed to wear a black armband to advertise his orphan status, and he enjoyed the 'social prestige' that this conferred.[3] The boys expressed their condolences with the phrase 'bad luck, Isherwood', but had no conception of grief, and if he 'happened to remember his loss and was moved to shed a few tears over it, that was something he had to cope with by himself' (*KF*, 501). His mother and the teachers at St Edmund's continually reproached him for being unworthy of the sacred memory of his 'hero-father'. All the people like Kathleen and the clergymen, politicians and journalists who promulgated the jingoistic lie *Dulce et decorum est pro patria mori*[4] crystallized into a collective foe he dubbed 'the others':

> Timidly and secretly at first, but with passion, with a rage against The Others which possessed him to the marrow of his bones, he rejected their Hero-Father. Such a rejection leads to a much larger one. By denying your duty toward the Hero-Father you deny the authority of the Flag, the Old School Tie, the Unknown Soldier, The Land That Bore You and the God of Battles. (*KF*, 502)

Despite the subversive, antisocial sentiments that smouldered in his heart, outwardly Isherwood remained a docile schoolboy who won prizes for Divinity, English and good conduct at St Edmund's.[5] In fact, as Katherine Bucknell points out, at the time Isherwood 'supported the empire and the war unquestioningly';[6] it was only later that he rebelled.

It was at St Edmund's that he first met W. H. Auden. Isherwood includes a lively portrait of him at this time in *Lions and Shadows* as Hugh Weston (a play on Auden's first and middle names, Wystan Hugh). The son of a doctor, Auden had studied sexual reproduction in the illustrated books in his father's library, and gleefully expounded the facts of life to the awestruck boys. 'I remember him', writes Isherwood,

> chiefly for his naughtiness, his insolence, his smirking tantalizing air of knowing disreputable and exciting secrets. With his hinted forbidden knowledge and stock of mispronounced scientific words, portentously uttered, he enjoyed among us, his semi-savage credulous schoolfellows, the status of a kind of witch-doctor. (*LS*, 135–6)

In 1919 Isherwood was admitted to Repton, a prestigious public school in Derbyshire, where he continued to excel in his favourite subjects. It was at Repton that he met Edward Upward, who fomented his spirit of rebellion. In *Lions and Shadows*, Isherwood writes of the Upward 'caricature' he calls Allen Chalmers:

> Never in my life have I been so strongly and immediately attracted to any personality, before or since. Everything about him appealed to me. He was a natural anarchist, a born romantic revolutionary . . . His natural hatred of all established authority impressed me greatly and I felt that it was a weakness in myself not to share it; to be guilty, indeed, of having sometimes kissed the rod. (*LS*, 8–9)

To judge from Upward's autobiographical novel *No Home but the Struggle* (1977), his animosity towards Repton and its traditions derived from his experience of fagging. At his public school, Upward's alter ego Alan Sebrill considers himself lucky that he has a lenient 'studyholder' who only beats him a couple of times a term. What galls him is the relentless vilification of the older 'fags' who deride him for being an 'incomp' who burns the porridge and does not perform his duties with the exacting precision and zeal expected of 'new bugs'. He is nicknamed 'Auntie Flo' by a boy called Buscarlett for his girlish good looks; indeed, Buscarlett stirs up the contempt of the other boys after Sebrill spurns his homosexual advances. In response, Sebrill decides that 'whatever the school upheld as wholesome ought to be detested by me'.[7] He seeks imaginative escape from the horrors of fagging through writing poetry and cultivates a 'cult of gloom' that celebrates unhappiness, death, unrequited love and so on, which was inspired by the lugubrious lyricism of Edgar Allan Poe and Sir Thomas Browne.

At this time, Isherwood was writing poems and short stories and was an eager convert to Upward's cult of gloom. 'Funny that we are both so preoccupied with cemeteries and charnel vaults', Upward remarked in a letter. 'However I am convinced that death is the sole object of life.'[8] Inspired by another Repton boy named Hector Wintle, who was writing a *Bildungsroman* titled *Donald Stanton*, Isherwood

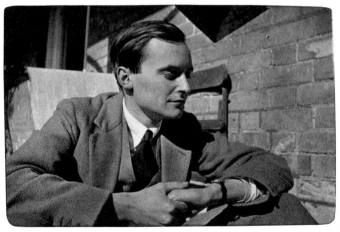

Edward Upward, taken by Isherwood at Freshwater Bay, Isle of Wight, May 1928.

embarked on a novel of his own. Isherwood and Upward were studying history with Graham Burrell Smith, a charismatic teacher who persuaded them to take scholarship exams to read history at Cambridge despite their literary ambitions. When they sat the exams at Corpus Christi, they conceived of themselves as spies venturing into the enemy camp. The Cambridge establishment became an extension of Repton and 'the others'. Thanks in part to Mr Smith, who advised them to memorize lines from Dante's *Inferno* in the original Italian and casually quote them in a plausible place in the exam, they both won scholarships.

By the time Isherwood went up to Cambridge in 1923, Upward, who was a year older, was in his second year. Clearly, they both needed each other to reinforce the adversarial fantasy of 'the others': Upward sheepishly admitted that he'd been playing football for Corpus Christi, which had involved a certain amount of patronage from the poshocracy. Meanwhile, as a freshman Isherwood was being courted by the poshocracy and had to pretend to despise them in front of Upward. Perhaps because of this mutual bad faith, they invented a character called 'The Watcher in Spanish', who would appear silently to signal their hypocrisy while, say, they flattered the poshocracy or a representative of the others. They invented several other characters and catchphrases for their fecund fantasy world, which they termed 'Mortmere'. 'Laily' (a word they seized on in a Scottish ballad, meaning hideous and loathsome) was by turns a flatulent don and a repellent 'swotter' and 'scholarship-hunter'. 'The combine' was another term for their enemies, which encompassed not just the dons and the poshocracy but the menial workers who silently participated in the academic 'blague', meaning an imposture or conspiracy.

One night on Garret Hostel Bridge, Upward exclaimed 'The Rats' Hostel', a cryptic phrase which came to signify many things, such as the medieval Gothic atmosphere they associated with the woodcuts of Albrecht Dürer, as well as embodying a counterforce to the combine, which included the ghosts of their favourite writers, namely Wilfred Owen, Katherine Mansfield and Emily Brontë. This need for a notional enemy and choosing between two Manichaean sides is common in adolescence, but was perhaps more pronounced in Isherwood's generation, who had grown up mentally preparing to fight in the First World War, only to find, when they came of age, that the conflict was over. It's no coincidence that Isherwood and Upward conceived of their campaign against the combine in military terms: 'We were going to open a monster offensive against the dons' (*LS*, 70).

Isherwood was a mediocre student, who couldn't concentrate in lectures and spent his time scrutinizing the other students and the tenebrous portraits of eminent dons. After a couple of weeks of feeling like a failure and panicking that he was being left behind, he stopped going to lectures altogether. With more time on his hands, he began to defy his puritan streak, drinking to excess and having sex with a couple of Cambridge men.[9] He also took up a novel he'd started writing that summer, titled 'Lions and Shadows' (this will be presented in quotation marks to differentiate it from the published memoir *Lions and Shadows*).[10] The protagonist, Leonard Merrows, comes down with rheumatic fever as he is about to enter Rugtonstead (an elite public school). As a result of his illness, he develops a cardiac condition which means that he is too delicate for the hurly-burly of public school and must continue his education with a private tutor at home. The novel was an expression of Isherwood's ambivalent feelings about the First World War, here symbolized by Rugtonstead. 'Like most of my generation,' he writes,

> I was obsessed by a complex of terrors and longings connected with the idea 'War.' 'War,' in this purely neurotic sense, meant The Test. The Test of your courage, of your maturity, of your sexual prowess: 'Are you really a Man?' Subconsciously, I believe, I longed to be subjected to this test; but I also dreaded failure. I dreaded failure so much – indeed, I was so certain that I *should* fail – that, consciously, I denied my longing to be tested, altogether. I denied my all-consuming morbid interest in the idea of 'war.' . . . The War, I said, was obscene, not even thrilling, a nuisance, a bore. (*LS*, 52)

It would have been appropriate, at this point in *Lions and Shadows*, to say something about the death of his father, but he ruthlessly excludes his family from the narrative. Isherwood was a talented pasticheur and described the style of 'Lions and Shadows' as a middlebrow mishmash of E. F. Benson, Compton Mackenzie and Hugh Walpole. While weeping over the purple passages in private, Isherwood was self-deprecating about his work in front of Upward, whose shaming critiques spurred him on to become a better, less derivative writer.

At Cambridge, Isherwood also worked with Upward on embellishing the Mortmere mythos. He wrote several stories featuring their alter egos, the pornographers Edward Hynd and Christopher Starn, who lived in the fantastic village of Mortmere. In French, the name denotes the death of mother, which is significant since both Isherwood and Upward harboured rancorous feelings towards their mothers.[11] Another allusion is to Marple Hall, which was named after a flooded valley in the vicinity called the Mere Pool. Thus Mortmere combined the death of Kathleen and Marple Hall, which embodied the past she venerated. As with the rats' hostel, Mortmere became an eccentric counterforce to Laily and the combine. 'Mortmere was a sort of anarchist paradise,' wrote Isherwood, 'in which all accepted moral and social values were turned upside down and inside out, and every kind of extravagant behaviour was possible and usual. It was our private place of retreat from the rules and conventions of university life.'[12]

The denizens of Mortmere were for the most part comic grotesques, designed to be shocking, subversive or sinister in a cartoonish way, such as the dastardly Reynard Moxon, the owner of a 'brothel for necrophiles' who attempts to steal the 'Javanese sapphires' with his pet python. Although Mortmere was a shared fantasy, they wrote the stories, poems and fragments independently, with each instalment enlarging the mythos. Isherwood's contributions owed a debt to Poe and to Conan Doyle's Sherlock Holmes stories.[13] For example, in 'The Horror in the Tower' the description of Lord Wranver's Gothic pile glimpsed by Starn in the gloaming reads like a parody of 'The Fall of the House of Usher'. Starn is instructed not to use the toilet at the top of the tower since it is haunted by one of Kester Wranver's demented forebears. But the ghost turns out to be Kester himself, who contrives somehow to place his head beneath the seat of the toilet in the tower and eat the falling excrement. 'In this instant of freezing horror,' Starn relates to Hynd, 'my sang-froid deserted me. I averted my eyes and fired, once, twice, three times, into the aperture,' killing Kester.[14] This was one of the few stories that was finished. Many existed only as intriguing titles: 'The Future of Love', 'Death's Other Kingdom', 'The Midnight Guest'.

In early 1925 Isherwood finished 'Lions and Shadows' and gave it to Ethel Mayne, an Irish novelist and family friend, whose tactful criticism persuaded him to drop it and start again. He was now in his second year at Cambridge, at the end of which he would have to sit the first part of the dreaded Tripos exam. He was too proud to settle for anything less than a First, and too realistic to imagine that he could attain this result through cramming. Furthermore, there was no incentive to try as Upward would graduate in the summer, leaving him to face the final year alone. So he resolved to get himself sent down by writing impertinent answers to the essay questions, and conceived of the enterprise as a witty insult to Laily and the combine. He wrote parts of the essays in verse and even contrived to include a sonnet on 'the causes of the Restoration'. When he tired of this, he poked fun at the questions and ended up deriding the decor of the examination hall. He made copies of his answers to show Upward, who excitedly proclaimed that Mortmere had won a decisive victory. According to Isherwood, 'failing the Tripos had merely been a kind of extension of dream-action on to the plane of reality,' but as he sat opposite his tutor, who was indignant that Isherwood had squandered his scholarship and wanted to know why, the baroque fantasy of Mortmere dissipated in the face of the prosaic, sternly adult world (*LS*, 97). With consternating clarity, he perceived that the tutor wasn't Laily but an innocuous middle-aged man and that his sophisticated answers to the Tripos questions, far from cocking a snook at the combine, were in fact puerile. Isherwood's Cambridge career, then, ended less with a triumphant bang than with a snigger.

2
Tea-Tabling, 1925–30

After being sent down from Cambridge in the summer of 1925, Isherwood purchased a roomy second-hand Renault, and cruised the streets of west London with Hector Wintle, the author of the abandoned Repton novel *Donald Stanton* who was now a medical student. Owning a car also came in handy with his new job as secretary to André Mangeot, the leader of the International String Quartet. Mangeot had an enormous backlog of unanswered letters concerning his quartet and Isherwood, having spent some months in Rouen after leaving Repton, was able to handle Mangeot's French correspondence.

Isherwood was enchanted with the Mangeot family; he favourably compared the bohemian chaos of their Kensington mews to the genteel tidiness of his mother's house in Olympia. Being an artist himself, Mangeot completely understood Isherwood's decision to drop out of Cambridge and pursue his literary bent, whereas Kathleen had wanted him to become an academic, or failing that to secure a respectable job with a good income, in contrast to the slender prospects of being secretary to a string quartet. Isherwood had a classic family romance with the Mangeots: the dashing André was the ideal bohemian father, while his English wife Olive was the glamorous, indulgent, artistically nurturing mother he felt he deserved. Although only employed for two hours a day, he contrived to spend as much time as possible with the family, eating meals with them and getting himself invited to concerts and the theatre. He jockeyed for position in the family as an honorary son and signed his letters to Olive 'your loving eldest, Christopher'.[1]

At Easter 1926 Isherwood and Upward took a holiday in the Scilly Isles. Upward had been working as a tutor in St Ives and had conceived of a new aesthetic technique he termed 'tea-tabling', which he'd discerned in the work of E. M. Forster. 'I saw it all suddenly while I was reading *Howards End*,' announces Chalmers in *Lions and Shadows*.

> Forster's the only one who understands what the modern novel ought to be . . . Our frightful mistake was that we believed in tragedy: the point is, tragedy's quite impossible nowadays . . . We ought to aim at being essentially comic writers . . . The whole of Forster's technique is based on the tea-table: instead of trying to screw all his scenes up to the highest possible pitch, he tones them down until they sound like mothers'-meeting gossip . . . In fact, there's actually *less* emphasis laid on the big scenes than on the unimportant ones: that's what's so utterly terrific. (*LS*, 128)

For example, in *Howards End* (1910), Mrs Wilcox dies off-stage; there's no dramatic death-bed scene, and the narrator begins the next chapter matter-of-factly: 'The funeral was over.'[2] Inspired by this new aesthetic, Isherwood and Upward sketched out the plot of what would become *All the Conspirators*, Isherwood's first published novel.

The previous Christmas, Isherwood had rekindled his friendship with Auden, whom he hadn't seen since his days at St Edmund's. After a pleasant afternoon of prep-school jokes and reminiscences, Auden announced that he was now writing poetry, and Isherwood condescendingly offered to read his stuff, expecting some illiterate tosh given that Auden had wanted to be a mining engineer at St Edmund's and was now reading Natural Science at Oxford. He was therefore surprised to discover that Auden's poetry was 'efficient, imitative and extremely competent', and was flattered that Auden deferred to his judgement, preserving only those lines that Isherwood liked and assembling whole poems from these disparate fragments, which contributed to the obscurity and difficulty of Auden's early work (*LS*, 138).[3] In July they went to Freshwater Bay on the Isle of

Wight, where it seems they began a sexual relationship that would persist, intermittently, for over a decade. Auden embarrassed him by wearing a preposterous black hat and loudly expounding his aesthetic theories in the pub. He had cast aside Thomas Hardy and Edward Thomas as poetic models in favour of the austere classicism of Eliot, but in place of erudite allusions to Dante and Chaucer, he lent his work a modernist opacity by using arcane scientific and psychoanalytic terminology.

Auden subjected Isherwood to long probing conversations about sex. In *Lions and Shadows*, written in the late 1930s, their sexual orientation is left ambiguous. Isherwood marvels at the Auden character's 'utter lack of inhibition' and broods on his sexual adventures (*LS*, 146). Auden aroused his 'nonconformist conscience' and, it is hinted, precipitated a crisis over his homosexuality. Isherwood shunned the company of the Mangeots and his friends, and took a comically dismal trip to Wales, where it rained continuously as he attempted to read Proust. In his diary, he reviled his character – alleging that he was 'a public lavatory that anyone might flush' (*LS*, 147). He made a dramatic will in which he instructed Upward to burn his manuscripts and diaries unread, and even went so far as to purchase a pistol, knowing that he lacked the courage to use it. Isherwood destroyed his diaries from this period and it's hard to trust the comic account he gives of this crisis in *Lions and Shadows*. For instance, he was probably employing artistic licence in the amusing dialogue he puts in the mouth of Philip Linsley (the Hector Wintle character), who advises Isherwood on the best technique to shoot himself: 'Better not try the heart, boy. Too risky. Stick it in your mouth, that's the best way' (*LS*, 147).

For all his emotional turmoil, he had managed to make some headway on the novel he'd conceived in the Scilly Isles, which he was calling *Seascape with Figures*. By October 1926 he'd finished a first draft, which he gave to Ethel Mayne, who encouraged him to send the manuscript to publishers. After two rejections, Isherwood decided to put the novel aside for six months. As was his wont, he immediately began plotting a new novel, which would be set in Cambridge, London, Wales and the Alps, grandly titled *The*

North-West Passage. The novel would illustrate the futile strivings of the 'Truly Weak Man', an important character type who would appear in much of Isherwood's early fiction, and who was the neurotic antithesis of the 'Truly Strong Man'.

These archetypes were inspired by a serial killer named Wagner, whom Isherwood had read about in Eugen Bleuler's *Textbook of Psychiatry* (1924). On the one hand, it seems significant that Isherwood was reading this book while grappling with conflicts arising from his sexuality;[4] on the other, both Upward and Isherwood became converts to psychoanalysis at Cambridge,[5] and Auden was independently reading Freud and Jung and would subsequently introduce Isherwood to the psychological theories of Homer Lane (discussed below).[6] In *Lions and Shadows*, Isherwood includes the following quote from Wagner:

> The feeling of impotence brings forth the strong words, the bold sounds to battle are emitted by the trumpet called persecution insanity. The signs of the truly strong are repose and good-will . . . the strong individuals are those who without any fuss do their duty. These have neither the time nor the occasion to throw themselves into a pose and try to be something great. (*LS*, 155–6).

What Isherwood inferred from this was that the truly strong man didn't need to test his courage and masculinity; 'the test', then, was for the truly weak man who must continually prove himself by going to war, or undertaking feats of derring-do such as the northwest passage from the Atlantic Ocean to the Pacific Ocean through the Arctic Archipelago, made famous by Roald Amundsen. What Isherwood neglects to mention is that Wagner thinks of himself as a weak man and in the ellipsis above he adds that the 'strong man, about whom we palaver in our literature, does not exist'.[7] And while Isherwood sketches out the plot of *The North-West Passage* in some detail in *Lions and Shadows*, he soon abandoned it.

To eke out his income as Mangeot's secretary, Isherwood became a private tutor. In *Lions and Shadows*, he reproduces his patter to prospective clients: 'Look here, Mrs Smith – will you let me talk to your son for five minutes, alone? Then, when I've gone, I want you to ask him if he'd like to have me for a tutor. It's no good whatever giving the boy a tutor he dislikes from the start' (*LS*, 150). The client would be so overcome by Isherwood's candour that even if the son disliked him, he would get the job. With the extra money he received from tutoring, in addition to his annual allowance of £150 (or £7,800 today),[8] Isherwood was able to move out of Kathleen's house into a nearby bedsit on Edith Grove in January 1927.[9] Despite the potpourri of bad smells that emanated from the kitchen, bathroom and stairs, Isherwood settled in quickly and began a new draft of *Seascape with Figures*. The previous summer, Isherwood had purchased a copy of *Ulysses* (1922) in Paris.[10] Under the influence of Joyce, he added several passages in the manner of Stephen Dedalus's stream of consciousness in the 'Proteus' chapter of *Ulysses*. Joyce was also responsible for Isherwood's new conception of the novelist as crafty artificer, who 'must continually amaze and deceive [the reader], with tricks, with traps, with extraordinary gambits, with sham climaxes, with false directions' (*LS*, 195). Consequently, Isherwood's novel was self-consciously modernist, and eschewed conventional exposition in favour of flashbacks, montage, interior monologues and cryptic dialogue untethered to a speaker. It was now called *All the Conspirators*; the new title was taken from Shakespeare's *Julius Caesar*, although the quotation ('All the conspirators save only he/ Did that they did in envy of great Caesar') had little bearing on the book.

    It begins *in medias res*, with the aspiring painter and poet Philip Lindsay arguing with his friend Allen Chalmers. Chalmers is a medical student like Hector Wintle, but his character was inspired by Upward, while Philip Lindsay, according to Isherwood, was based on Wintle.[11] Granted, Wintle was also an aspiring writer who, like Lindsay, had suffered rheumatic fever as a boy, and his parents' house in North Kensington is the model for the Lindsays' house in Bellingham Gardens.[12] Inevitably, though, there are autobiographical elements in Isherwood's portrait of an aspiring writer who lives with his widowed mother in west London.

Lindsay is a truly weak man who, like the protagonist of Isherwood's previous novel 'Lions and Shadows', contracted rheumatic fever as a boy, and so failed the test of public school and had to be educated by private tutors instead. Rather than going to university, he has spent the past four years working in an insurance office, and is now attempting the test of becoming an artist. At the start of the novel, Lindsay has just quit his job and fled to the Scilly Isles with Chalmers. They argue about a poshocrat from Chalmers's public school called Victor Page, who is coincidentally staying at their hotel. The home-schooled Lindsay lacks Chalmers's visceral loathing of the poshocracy, and speaks to Page that night in the smoking room, who confides that he grows 'frightfully morbid' if he doesn't get 'heaps of fresh air and exercise', and disapproves of 'super-aesthetes' (AC, 24). But where Chalmers fulminates at this kind of thing, Lindsay regards Page as a basically decent (if philistine) fellow, and they promise to keep in touch.

At this point, Chalmers bursts into the smoking room, clearly drunk, and has to be escorted to his room by Page and Lindsay. One critic has suggested that there is a covert homosexual attraction between Page and Lindsay, and that Chalmers is jealous and creates a scene to disrupt their burgeoning intimacy.[13] The next day, Lindsay is so mortified by Chalmers's behaviour that he insists they leave the hotel and go back to London without even having breakfast, not wanting to face Page and his uncle. Another explanation for Chalmers's behaviour is that he is suffering from a pathological boredom he likens to a cancer, and cannot bear the thought of spending another fortnight in the Scilly Isles bickering with Lindsay.

Back in London, Lindsay confronts his mother, who is dismayed that he has quit his respectable office job to pursue his art, while Lindsay is offended by her bourgeois mistrust of his vocation. One of the chief differences between Lindsay and his creator is that, where Isherwood actually was an artist who had already written reams of fiction by Lindsay's age, Lindsay is a dilettante, and during the next few days he is unable to finish a painting or make any progress on his novel. Frustrated with sitting in his room all day pretending to work, Lindsay writes to Mr Langbridge, a stockbroker friend of the family, for advice; Mr Langbridge adopts the conventional bourgeois line that writing and painting are hobbies that can be practised at the weekend, and pulls some strings to restore Lindsay's job at the insurance office.

Meanwhile, Page has visited the house in Bellingham Gardens. Mrs Lindsay is impressed by his wealth and manners, encourages her daughter Joan to accept his subsequent invitations to play tennis, and within a few months Page has proposed. In a dizzying modernist montage, Page recalls a cryptic sermon about masturbation and a fervent friendship with a boy called Basley at public school. These memories are interspersed with poshocrat comments about psychoanalysis, repression, compulsions and 'tricky complexes'. Perhaps as a consequence, he conceives of Joan as a jolly female pal with whom he can play games and gets flustered when she kisses him. If Page is heterosexual, then his experience with Basley and the sermons on masturbation have made him ashamed of any kind of sexual feelings. At the time, it wasn't unusual for public-school boys to develop platonic crushes on younger boys, but then to have relationships with women as adults. At Repton, for example, Upward fell in love with a boy named Gibbens, but wanted nothing more than to hold his hand, and his subsequent sexual experiences were all with women.[14] Furthermore, marrying Joan will provide Page with a family, for both his parents are dead and he lives with a starchy military uncle.

Lindsay's sexual orientation is less ambiguous. At the insurance office in the summer, he cannot bear 'the aroma of the girls' increased sexual vitality', and he takes umbrage when Chalmers suggests that he eat 'steak and stout' instead of 'sugary puddings' and take up boxing (*AC*, 96, 104). When Lindsay complains that his job is tedious and that he longs for fresh air in the 'stuffy atmosphere' of the office, Page uses his connections to find him a job on a coffee plantation in Kenya. The owner's descriptions of the hearty plantation life – lots of hard work and sport and no privacy whatsoever – do nothing to deter Lindsay, and he ignores the protests of Chalmers and Joan, who predict that he will hate it. The Kenya job, then, is another version of the test that Lindsay, the 'truly weak man', will inevitably fail. The day before his departure, he flees Bellingham Gardens, forgetting his coat, and comes down with another bout of rheumatic fever, which had previously served to save him from the test of public school and now effectively prevents him from going to Kenya.

In the aftermath, the whole household mollycoddles Lindsay and more effort is made to encourage his artistic efforts. He sells some watercolours in a local bazaar and one of his poems wins second prize in a newspaper competition. These 'artistic successes', though, indicate the middlebrow nature of Lindsay's work. In a 1958 foreword, Isherwood described the novel as a depiction of 'the great war between the old and the young',[15] and Alan Wilde has argued that Mrs Lindsay's rejuvenated appearance while she tends to her infantilized son represents a triumph of the old guard.[16] In a lecture from the late 1950s, Isherwood affirmed that in his first novel, he was

> writing fundamentally about the Freudian revolution which had just hit England with tremendous force. It was, of course, the greatest literary event of my time . . . it's almost impossible to imagine the excitement with which we received the news that our parents were responsible for absolutely everything. It was all their fault, and we would never, never forgive. And what's more, all of the things that they said about morality and life were wrong and exploded and out of date.[17]

But this retrospective assessment seems out of kilter with the actual text. For the young characters are scarcely Freudian revolutionaries: Lindsay unthinkingly endorses his mother's bourgeois morality by, for example, leaving the hotel in the Scillies when Chalmers makes a minor scene; Page sublimates his sexuality in sport and can barely bring himself to kiss his fiancée; and Chalmers, for all his rebellious hatred of the poshocracy, is studying to be a doctor and is too timid to act on his desire for Joan. At the conclusion of the novel, we find Lindsay in bed wearing mittens in case he gets a chill, lecturing Chalmers to be less 'timid' and more venturesome. Conversely, what Isherwood may be suggesting in the quotation above is that the older generation, by ruthlessly reinforcing the superegos of their children, has crippled the pleasure principle.

After finishing his final draft of *All the Conspirators* at Freshwater Bay in July 1927, Isherwood entered a restless period while his manuscript did the rounds of the publishers. The stench of the house on Edith Grove depressed him, and when an Irish couple absconded with his gramophone, he decided to move back home. With no tutoring work on the horizon, and nothing but rejections from the publishers, Isherwood resolved to become a doctor. The idea had been suggested by a war veteran he had met at Freshwater Bay (and who appears as Lester in *Lions and Shadows*).[18] Kathleen was delighted at the idea of her son embarking on a respectable career, while Upward invoked Chekhov as an example of a successful writer and doctor; only Hector Wintle, who knew what was involved, tried to dissuade him.

Isherwood was too late to enrol for the new cohort of medical students in 1927, which meant he had time to embark on a new novel. Where *Ulysses* was the key influence on *All the Conspirators*, which was finally accepted by Jonathan Cape in January 1928, *War and Peace* was the book that inspired his second novel, *The Memorial*. 'It was to be about war,' writes Isherwood: 'not the War itself, but the effect of the idea of "War" on my generation. It was to give expression, at last, to my own "War" complex' (*LS*, 224). Meanwhile, *All the Conspirators* was published in May 1928. Although the novel would later be praised by Cyril Connolly and Hugh Walpole, the press reviews were barbed.[19] 'Mr Christopher Isherwood', wrote the critic in *Punch*, 'is either badly troubled with that kind of portentous solemnity which so often accompanies the mental growing pains of the very young, or else he has written his novel with his tongue in his cheek . . . Altogether, the book leaves behind it a faintly nasty taste.'[20] In contrast, Kathleen was proud of her son's achievement and noted in her diary that the novel was 'very interesting & a clever study of a family we know' (in other words, her own).[21]

In his final year at Oxford, Auden had befriended an aspiring writer named Stephen Spender, who was reading Philosophy, Politics and Economics at University College. He gave Isherwood one of Spender's stories to read, and Isherwood immediately perceived the author's potential and agreed to meet him. 'He burst in upon us, blushing, sniggering loudly, contriving to trip over the edge of the carpet,' writes Isherwood; 'an immensely tall, shambling boy of nineteen, with a great scarlet poppy-face, wild frizzy hair, and eyes the violent colour of bluebells' (*LS*, 212). Moments later, they were all laughing and joshing and talking too loudly. In his memoir, *World within World* (1951), Spender recalls the meeting differently, with Isherwood and Auden ignoring him until Isherwood had finished critiquing one of Auden's poems. Where, for Spender, Auden was the 'highest peak' of literary eminence, 'for Auden there was another peak, namely Isherwood, whilst for Isherwood there was a still further peak, Chalmers' (that is, Upward).[22] As with Auden, Isherwood acted as a literary mentor to Spender, dispensing manfully disinterested, faintly patronizing advice, and was only too happy to encourage Spender's puppyish hero worship.

In October 1928 Isherwood began his medical studies at King's College London. Given his academic ineptitude at Cambridge, it came as no surprise that he was even more maladroit when it came to physics and chemistry, which he'd barely touched on at Repton. He was six years older than most of the students, and 'felt like a man of forty' in comparison (*LS*, 215). This time Isherwood did at least try to study, which made his failure more ignominious. His only consolation was *The Memorial*, which he would work on in the late afternoons once his lectures were over. He wrote with unprecedented fluency, and by December he had finished a first draft.

Since graduating from Oxford in the summer of 1928, Auden had been living in Berlin, in a pointed attempt to buck the trend of apprentice poets who flocked to Paris in search of inspiration.[23] Back in England for Christmas, he caught up with Isherwood, who was excited to hear of Auden's sexual exploits in the proletarian Hallesches Tor district, where the rent boys were plentiful and cheap. Whatever qualms Auden might have felt about paying for sex had been dissipated by the anthropologist John Layard, whom he had met in Berlin.[24] A few years earlier, Layard had suffered a debilitating depression and had been referred to an American psychologist named Homer Lane, who was then practising in England. After his therapist's death in 1925, Layard became the chief exponent of Lane's ideas. What appealed to Auden, and especially Isherwood, about Lane's psychology was his doctrine of original virtue, which held that humans were innately good rather than innately wicked. Lane's theories involved a Nietzschean transvaluation of Christian morality: God was an emblem of the id, whose impulses should be obeyed, whereas the Devil represented the ego and the superego, who policed desire with the stick of rectitude and reason. Following Nietzsche, Lane reviled the Christian virtues of humility, pity and forbearance. The only sin for Lane was repressing one's instincts, which resulted in insanity or illness. In this manner, all disease was psychosomatic and was indicative of a 'sickness of the soul' rather than an infirmity of the body. Cancer, Lane held, was the result of thwarted creativity; syphilis was caused by 'sexual guilt'; tuberculosis 'represented a desire to return to early childhood' (*LS*, 229).

While Isherwood was initially sceptical of Lane's ideas, they made him reflect on the reasons why he'd chosen to study medicine, and he perceived that becoming a doctor was another way of shirking the test: both the test of war (doctors were exempt from military service) and the test of literature (with a medical degree he would become a dilettante). The voice of reason (the Devil in Lane's schema) told him to stick to his medical studies; however, this was nothing but fear of his deepest desire (Lane's God) to drop out, 'to shock Mummy and Daddy and Nanny, to smash the nursery clock, to be a really naughty little boy' (*LS*, 232). Shortly afterwards, he announced his intention of quitting medical school, and, as a sop to Kathleen, agreed to see out the next term, which had been paid for in advance.

Lions and Shadows culminates with Isherwood embarking for Berlin on 14 March 1929, eagerly anticipating his meeting with Barnard (his name for Layard). In *Christopher and His Kind*, however, he alters the emphasis: 'It was Berlin itself he was hungry to meet; the Berlin Wystan had promised him. To Christopher, Berlin meant Boys' (*CK*, 3). Nonetheless, Lane's thesis that humans should heed their innermost desires, ignoring the strictures of conventional morality, must have smoothed the way for Isherwood's impassioned affair with a rent boy named Bubi (Berthold Szczesny) whom he met in a bar called the Cosy Corner.

In England, Isherwood's sexual encounters had been marred by what Freud termed the virgin-whore complex, in which heterosexual men found their respectable wives erotically lifeless and sought out prostitutes to satisfy their base desires. For homosexuals such as Isherwood, this meant that 'he couldn't relax sexually with a member of his own class or nation' and required instead 'a working-class foreigner' (CK, 3). This 'inhibition' is presumably what had vitiated his affair with Auden. For his part, Auden was in love with Isherwood, and felt envious of Bubi, despite having facilitated the relationship by taking Isherwood to the Cosy Corner.[25] With his blond hair, blue eyes and hard boxer's body, Bubi appeared to Isherwood to be an archetypal German boy (though he was actually Czech). Like many of the rent boys at the Cosy Corner, Bubi was mostly heterosexual and spent his money on female prostitutes. 'Christopher wanted to keep Bubi all to himself forever, to possess him utterly,' Isherwood writes, 'and he knew that this was impossible and absurd. If he had been a savage, he might have solved the problem by eating Bubi – for magical, not gastronomic, reasons' (CK, 5).

On his return, Isherwood took a tutoring job with a boy called Wallace Lanigan, in Bettyhill, Scotland. The mother was either widowed or divorced and not much older than Isherwood. 'After dark, in that tiny place,' he writes, 'there was nothing social to do but play cards, get drunk, or make love' (CK, 11). And so Isherwood made love with Mrs Lanigan, adapting the techniques he'd learned from Bubi to a female body, and finding himself 'genuinely aroused', less by the charms of Mrs Lanigan than by observing the effect he was having on her. The lovemaking seems to have taken place in the living room, for when Isherwood invited Mrs Lanigan to repair to his bedroom, so that they might enjoy each other's bodies without the encumbrance of clothes, it was Mrs Lanigan who belatedly developed scruples and declined. There would be no repeat performance, and Isherwood was fired after less than a month.[26]

At the end of November 1929 Isherwood moved to Berlin for an indefinite stay. Auden was now living in England and the only person Isherwood knew was one of his friends, Francis Turville-Petre, a dissolute archaeologist who was being treated for syphilis at the Institut für Sexualwissenschaft (Institute for Sexual Science) established by the sexologist Magnus Hirschfeld. Through Turville-Petre, Isherwood became acquainted with Karl Giese, Hirschfeld's secretary and partner, who gave him a guided tour of the institute's museum. He was at once titillated, embarrassed and repelled by the exhibits, which included fetish objects and BDSM paraphernalia, erotic artwork from the patients, and photographs of hermaphrodite genitalia and famous homosexuals, such as Oscar Wilde and Walt Whitman. Despite regarding himself as the gadfly of bourgeois respectability, Isherwood was shocked when he registered that a fellow diner at the institute was a cross-dresser. Hitherto, he had behaved as if homosexuality were a coterie quirk of Auden and his friends, and it discomfited him 'to admit kinship with these freakish fellow tribesmen and their distasteful customs' (CK, 16–17). Hirschfeld had founded the institute in 1919 in the hope of lending dignity and scientific respectability to the study of homosexuality, which, *pace* Krafft-Ebing and Freud, he did not regard in terms of degeneration or disorder.[27]

Now that he was settled in Berlin, in an apartment near the institute, Isherwood began revising *The Memorial* in a nearby café in the mornings. He would drink beer and smoke as he worked on the new draft. The beer made him less inhibited until around the fourth glass, when it began to hinder his judgement, at which point he would head home to have lunch with Turville-Petre (who lived in the same apartment). 'This is what freedom is,' he reflects. 'This is how I ought always to have lived' (CK, 23). Turville-Petre was the model for the character of Ambrose in *Down There on a Visit*. He regarded syphilis as a homosexual badge of honour and was faintly contemptuous of those cowards – Isherwood among them – who took prophylactic measures against the disease. Now that his syphilis was no longer infectious, Turville-Petre conducted Isherwood around his favourite boy bars in the Hallesches Tor. On the one hand,

Isherwood exhibited admirable restraint, abandoning Turville-Petre long before his 'Journey to the End of the Night' so he could work on *The Memorial* in the morning (CK, 29). On the other hand, he did not stint himself when it came to rent boys, and boasted to a correspondent: 'I am doing what Henry James would have done, if he had had the guts' (CK, 32).

Isherwood could afford to write full time with a small allowance from Uncle Henry, whose favour he had been courting since Henry had inherited the Isherwood estate in 1924. In a spirit of gratitude for the allowance, Isherwood was expected to regale his uncle with salacious stories over dinner, which would culminate in 'a goodnight kiss which was too warm and searching for any nephew, even one's favourite' (KF, 493). When Isherwood's quarterly allowance was not paid in February 1930, he returned to London to investigate. There he discovered that Kathleen and his younger brother Richard were at loggerheads over the latter's future. Richard had what would now be termed learning difficulties and had been sent to several specialist schools over the years, only to abscond from them and return to Kathleen. Now eighteen, Richard was refusing to retake the entrance exams for St John's College, Oxford, which he'd failed the previous year. Inevitably, Isherwood took his brother's side against Kathleen, framing the situation in terms of his personal mythos:

> She had tried to turn Christopher into a Cambridge don, he said, to gratify her selfish daydream of the kind of son she wanted him to be. And since he had foiled her, by getting himself thrown out of college, she was trying to turn Richard into an Oxford don, against his will. (CK, 38–9)

The idea that either Isherwood or his brother could have become a don is preposterous; Isherwood seems to imagine that it was only by his heroic ruse of failing his exams that he escaped the ivory tower of academia. In retaliation, Isherwood told his mother about his sex life in Berlin. Kathleen was nonplussed by his descriptions: 'How could there be real sex without women?' (CK, 39). In the end,

Isherwood was unable to secure that quarter's allowance, and returned to Berlin in May.

Shortly afterwards, he started seeing a teenage boy named Walter Wolff, who would inspire the character of Otto Nowak in *Goodbye to Berlin*. Walter had much in common with his predecessor Bubi – they were both muscular narcissistic boys who slept with men but preferred women and expected gifts and money in return. In *Christopher and His Kind*, Isherwood reveals that where 'Isherwood' in *Goodbye to Berlin* goes to live with the Nowak family in the autumn of 1931 because he has been impoverished by the fall in sterling following Britain's abandonment of the Gold Standard, he actually decided to move in with Walter's family in the Simeonstrasse the year before because Walter suggested it, and Isherwood felt that the experience of slumming it would be a 'thrilling adventure'. Likewise, the communist sympathies that 'Isherwood' exhibits in *Goodbye to Berlin* had much to do with his sexual predilection for working-class boys. 'The fact was that Christopher, the upper-class boy, was now trying to disown his class,' writes Isherwood. 'Because he hated it, he despised the middle class for aping its ways. That left him with nothing to admire but the working class; so he declared it to be forthright, without frills, altogether on the path of truth' (CK, 26). Where the Nazis attacked homosexuals and insisted that 'Germany must be virile,'[28] Upward (a recent communist convert) assured him: 'As far as I know Lenin said nothing about buggery. Possibly there wasn't any in Russia . . . In any case persecution of buggers is anti-Leninist.'[29]

The Wolff family consisted of Walter's parents, a twelve-year-old sister and an older brother, who all lived in a one-bedroom flat in a slum tenement that had been condemned as unfit by the housing authorities. There were two double beds in the living room, which barely left room for the table on which they ate their meals, a tiny kitchen with a pungent sink in which the family washed themselves, and a communal toilet shared with three other flats. As a paying lodger, Isherwood occupied the only bedroom with Walter, forcing his twenty-year-old brother to share a bed with his sister in the living room next door. While Isherwood was able to spritz his charm on Walter's parents and sister, the older brother was a Nazi who regarded him with contempt. Isherwood's spartan lifestyle only fanned the flames of Spender's hero worship: 'His renunciation of England, his poverty, his friendship, his independence, his work, all struck me as heroic. During months in the winter of 1930, when I went back to England, I corresponded with him in the spirit of writing letters to a Polar explorer.'[30] Isherwood made a point of eating in cheap restaurants and stoically partaking of the proletarian diet of 'horse flesh and lung soup', while spending the money he saved on gifts for Walter.[31]

Similarly, in *Goodbye to Berlin*, Isherwood portrays himself as a correspondent writing dispatches from the poverty line. In one scene, the narrator is sitting at the cramped living-room table with the Nowak family on a dismal Sunday afternoon; he is ostensibly trying to work on *The Memorial*, but finding the drama of its upper-class English characters artificial in comparison to the gritty authenticity of the lumpenproletariat in Berlin. In *Christopher and His Kind*, Isherwood lampoons the hypocrisy of his younger self; after quoting from the scene above, he writes:

> here 'Isherwood' is playing to the gallery . . . 'Isherwood,' merely because he has moved to the Simeonstrasse, feels that he has broken with his bourgeois literary past. Anything written about the upper classes is simply not worth reading, he implies. The rich *ought* to be happy . . . since they are living on money they've stolen from the poor; if they are miserable, that's just too tiresome. In any case, their lives can never be meaningful, as the lives of the Nowaks are – and as 'Isherwood's' life is, now that he is living with them. (CK, 53–4)

Unsurprisingly, the thrill of slumming it soon began to pall, and Isherwood's stay with the Wolffs lasted little more than a month. After a brief interlude in another slum district, he moved to the more affluent area of Schöneberg in December 1930, where he took a room in an apartment at Nollendorfstrasse 17. His landlady, Frl. Meta Thurau, was the model for Frl. Schroeder, who appears in both *Mr Norris Changes Trains* and *Goodbye to Berlin*. Moreover, the characters of Sally Bowles, Mr Norris and Bobby the barman all originated in people Isherwood encountered at Frl. Thurau's. And it was in his room at Frl. Thurau's that Isherwood finally finished his third draft of *The Memorial* in December 1930.

Like *War and Peace*, the novel is divided into four books, but where Tolstoy's narrative is chronological and inexorably builds towards the French invasion of Russia, Isherwood tea-tables the First World War and explores its aftermath on the Vernon family. The idea was to avoid the longueurs of the epic, such as the protagonist's childhood and Tolstoy's disquisitions on history, by presenting the 'story in self-contained scenes, like a play; an epic in an album of snapshots'. The narrative starts in 1928, then travels backwards and forwards and culminates in 1929, thereby suggesting that 'time is circular, which sounds Einstein-ish and brilliantly modern' (*LS*, 225). In fact, what Einstein argued was that the past, present and future co-existed, whereas Isherwood's circular time scheme suggests a more classical message: you cannot escape the past. His treatment of time may have been influenced by Virginia Woolf, whose novel *To the Lighthouse* (1927) also tea-tables the war and features time jumps between the different sections. But in *The Memorial* Isherwood's influences have been artfully incorporated, in contrast to the sub-Joycean streams of consciousness in *All the Conspirators*. In *The Memorial*, Isherwood elevates his war complex from the personal to the universal, and galvanizes theme, structure and style to present an elegiac vision of post-war England.

On the one hand, Eric Vernon shares certain attributes with Isherwood without being conventionally autobiographical. He is the same age and feels ashamed for not having fought in the First World War; his father Richard died in the conflict and this has driven a wedge between himself and his mother Lily, who reveres the past, symbolized by the Hall, the Vernon family seat in Cheshire; he despises Cambridge, with its roistering poshocrats, and drops out to spite his mother's wish that he become a don. On the other hand, Eric thinks of himself as ugly, is socially inept and harbours no artistic ambitions; at Cambridge he works hard and is a brilliant scholar; he is also wealthy, having inherited the Hall and the Vernon estate following the death of his grandfather.

The set-piece of the novel occurs in Book Two (set in 1920 when Eric is seventeen), with the church service at Chapel Bridge to commemorate the fallen soldiers of the war and the laying of wreaths at the foot of the Memorial Cross. Isherwood's portrait of Lily is more nuanced and empathetic than Mrs Lindsay in *All the Conspirators*, chiefly because he allows the reader access to her thoughts in the form of interior monologues. As she travels to the church with Eric and her father-in-law John Vernon, she recalls her first visit to the Hall, which was based on Marple Hall, and her delight with the architecture and the trappings and the deference of the servants. While Lily is a little too pleased that 'her eyes look extraordinarily lost and tragic' through the veil of her hat, there is no gainsaying the sincerity of her grief (*M*, 71). Eric learns of his father's death at school, and for a few weeks he is 'almost intolerably unhappy', but as the term passes there comes a point when 'he knew that he could bear it'; thus he returns home for the Easter holidays expecting a resumption of normality and is humbled by the spectacle of Lily's suffering:

> For a moment, he hardly recognised Lily. She was hideous with grief. Her eyes swollen into slits, her mouth heavy and pouting, her face blotched and sallow. He hung back, scared. The smile shrank from his lips. She gave a kind of hoarse cry. He rushed into her arms. That was agony. He knew then that everything he'd imagined he'd suffered at school was nothing, mere selfishness, triviality. She reopened the wound and tore it ten times wider. And now it would have made no difference to Eric if ten fathers had been killed. It was only for her he felt. Father was dead. But she was alive and suffering like this under his very eyes. He could do absolutely nothing. (*M*, 151–2)

After the death of her husband, Lily becomes fossilized in the pre-war past, the prelapsarian period when Richard was alive; as a result, she loses contact with Eric, who feels he cannot share his inner world with her any more, and that the vagaries of his life are overshadowed by her grief. Lily inwardly revolts at the rude incursions of the present, such as the 'new sanatorium' for tubercular children in Manchester that spoils the view from her bedroom window, and the rash of 'hideous' bungalows that have sprung up like toadstools in Chapel Bridge. Having married into the landed gentry, Lily is a ferocious snob, and is indignant that the officers' names are not read first at the church service, and that the names of the fallen are stripped of their rank on the Memorial Cross.

At the service, Lily spots her sister-in-law Mary Scriven, who was based on Olive Mangeot. Mary's husband was a philandering musician, and she does not mourn his death in the war. 'All this cult of dead people is only snobbery,' she reflects, as she contemplates the Memorial Cross. 'So much so, that the attitude which we're all subscribing to at this moment seems to me not only false but, yes, actually wicked. Living people are better than dead ones. And we've got to get on with life' (*M*, 112–13). On the surface, Mary seems to be the opposite of Lily, a representative of life rather than death, who shrugs off her fallen husband and provides for her children, Maurice and Anne, by running a restaurant, which also serves as a concert and gallery space; thus Eric regards her as a surrogate mother. After the service, Eric tries to console Lily but perceives that there is nothing he can do to help, and cycles to the 'positive pole' of Gatesley to be with Mary and his cousins. As he approaches, he sees them all having a good time in the garden: Maurice, on whom he has a crush, is playing hockey with some boys. Also present is Richard's friend Edward Blake, a decorated war hero whom Maurice idolizes. When the middle-aged Blake starts roughhousing with Maurice on the lawn, Eric grows jealous. Much as he longs to join this pageantry of the present at Gatesley, Eric feels himself an outsider and symbolically turns back towards the 'negative pole' of Chapel Bridge, his mother and the past.

In Book Three, set in 1925, Eric is a sedulous history student at Cambridge, while Maurice has taken after his father and become a charming ne'er-do-well, who crashes other people's cars, runs up debts and does no academic work. Maurice's profligacy is abetted by the independently wealthy Blake. Like Lily, Blake is trapped in the past by his love for Richard, and, though it's never stated, his attraction to boys may derive from the imago of Richard at public school. There are shades of Edward Upward in Blake, who rages against the indignity and injustice of fagging, and dares refuse no test or challenge from the school fellows he despises in a desperate bid to prove himself. Blake is thus positioned as the truly weak man who is in thrall to the truly strong man, Richard: 'Richard's strength and calm made [Blake] conscious of his own weakness . . . Richard had no need to give proofs of his courage, to assert the strength of his will. He was sure of himself – therefore he did not have to fight and boast' (*M*, 133). After Eric persuades Blake to stay away from Maurice, Blake has a string of unhappy affairs with young men and eventually travels to Berlin, where he shoots himself in the head, but miraculously survives. As unlikely as this sounds, Isherwood based this episode on the suicide attempt of John Layard, who apparently shot a bullet through the roof of his mouth into his nose, then went to see Auden and begged him to finish the job.[32]

Even in Book Two, the old social order is beginning to collapse. The squire of Chapel Bridge, the dotard John Vernon, who drools and has trouble speaking as the result of a stroke, is regarded by the villagers at the service as a curious relic from the past. 'Landowners were becoming obsolete,' Mary Scriven reflects. 'Father was obsolete. The vehicle he sat in was obsolete . . . His present claim on their attention was chiefly that, by a sort of accident, he happened to be not yet dead' (*M*, 124). In Book Four, Eric has sold the Hall to a nouveau riche industrialist and his social-climbing second wife, who will use it as a status symbol, while residing elsewhere. Mary, taking a valedictory look around the Hall, reflects: 'the house was quite dead. It had died of neglect. It was a show place, like all the others' (*M*, 246).

As if in penance for his inherited wealth, Eric spends his money on 'Communistic schemes', such as charity for unemployed miners in South Wales and a club for working-class boys. Despite Eric's efforts to escape the past, all his actions – dropping out of Cambridge, selling the Hall, his charity work – are a reaction against Lily, and are thus conditioned by his father's death. While Blake seeks a sort of redemption in volunteering for Eric's boys' club, at the end of the novel he has taken up with another young man, condemned by Richard's death to repeat the same cycle. Even Mary, for all her affirmation of the living, is haunted by the past. At the memorial service, she reflects that she despises men, and is unable to have a relationship because of her dead husband's adultery. She is repeatedly asked to do her impression of Queen Victoria, and at the end of the novel she swears that this is her 'very last performance', but the reader suspects she will have to act out the past again and again.[33]

Paradoxically, the only flaw in the novel is Isherwood's portrayal of Eric, who comes to life as an awkward, stammering adolescent, but as an adult he is a sketchy figure, and both his philanthropic activities and his sexual identity remain vague.[34] Eric's feelings for Maurice suggest that he is homosexual, but at a party in Book One he becomes enflamed by the 'half-naked body' of Priscilla Gore-Eckersley and 'Naomi, the less subtle whore' (*M*, 41). Granted, Eric could be bisexual, but his adventitious desire for Priscilla and Naomi seems unconvincing. In the final scene of the novel, Blake reads a letter from Eric in which he announces that he is going to become a Catholic. While many homosexuals at that time, such as Uncle Henry, combined an active sex life with Catholicism, one feels that Eric wants to sublimate his sexuality. For Alan Wilde, Eric's embrace of the Catholic Church is indicative of his capitulation to 'authority', to the 'negative pole' of Chapel Bridge and the past; the enemy forces against which he'd attempted to revolt.[35]

As with *All the Conspirators*, the novel ends ironically. Blake's German boyfriend Franz asks him where he got the scar on his head and doesn't believe him when he says he tried to commit suicide; eventually, Blake acquiesces in the lie that he got it in the war. '"You know," said Franz, very serious and evidently repeating something he had heard said by his elders: "that War . . . it ought never to have happened"' (*M*, 294).

3
The Lost, 1931–7

When Upward read the manuscript of *The Memorial*, he proclaimed: 'All delays, destructions, boys, pangs, debauches, are now totally justified . . . All that remains is to rewrite War and Peace.'[1] Isherwood seems to have taken this jocular suggestion to heart, for he began to contemplate an epic novel about Berlin that he would grandly title *The Lost*. It would present a series of character sketches based on the people Isherwood had met against the backdrop of the unravelling Weimar Republic.

One of these Berlin characters was Jean Ross. Writing in 1976, Isherwood confessed that he was unable to disentangle Ross from the Sally Bowles of *Goodbye to Berlin* (1939) and the various actresses who'd taken on the role in the play *I Am a Camera* (1951) by John van Druten and the musical *Cabaret* (1966), both of which were made into films.[2] Like Sally, Ross had come to Berlin in the hope of acquiring acting work and had become a cabaret performer, whose chutzpah compensated for her poor singing. She met Isherwood through another lodger at Frl. Thurau's, Franz von Ullmann, a Hungarian businessman who would serve as the model for Fritz Wendel in *Goodbye to Berlin*, and Ross moved into a vacant room at Nollendorfstrasse 17 shortly afterwards. Much of Ross's background makes its way into Isherwood's portrait of Sally, such as pretending to be pregnant in order to get expelled from school. She briefly attended RADA and was evidently a more talented actor than Sally for she obtained some film work and was given a part in a London production of the Ibsen play *Peer Gynt*.[3]

Perhaps taking her cue from Isherwood and the homosexual Ullmann, Ross claimed to have many, many lovers, most of whom Isherwood assumed were imaginary, though in retrospect he felt she might not have been exaggerating.[4] Ross became pregnant by a Jewish musician named Götz von Eick, and underwent a back-street abortion in the summer of 1931. Eick changed his name to Peter van Eyck and moved to Hollywood, where he made his name by playing Nazis. Tennessee Williams described him as '*excruciatingly* beautiful' and the 'most exciting man I have ever looked at'.[5] Sally's surname was suggested by the American composer and novelist Paul Bowles, who had come to Berlin to study with Aaron Copland and would often have lunch with Isherwood. In his memoirs, Bowles recalled visits to Frl. Thurau's, where he would find Ross 'stretched out in

Jean Ross, *c.* 1931, taken by Lady Spencer.

bed, smoking Murattis and eating chocolates', surrounded by German suitors.⁶

Another Berlin character Isherwood met around this time was the conman Gerald Hamilton. He immediately recognized Hamilton's literary potential, and fictionalized him as the affable rogue Arthur Norris. Hamilton liked to present himself as the descendant of Irish landowners in County Tyrone, but his father was a Scottish businessman who was based in London. After attending Rugby, Hamilton travelled extensively on a small allowance, and inveigled his way into high society. In *Christopher and His Kind*, Isherwood quotes from *Mr Norris and I* (1956), an autobiography Hamilton wrote to capitalize on his literary fame, in which he boasts of being interned during the First World War for his 'anti-British sentiments'. In fact, his first stint in prison was for gross indecency with soldiers; he was then 'interned on suspicion of pro-German sympathies' until the end of the war.⁷ He was a man of contradictions: a staunch republican and fawning royalist, a pacifist and gun-runner for the IRA, a Roman Catholic and communist sympathizer. Isherwood opined that were it not for his cautious nature he might have been sucked into one of Hamilton's illegal schemes.

In 1931 Isherwood, Walter Wolff and Spender took a summer holiday in Sellin, a resort town on the German island of Rügen, where they were joined by Auden. Both Isherwood and Spender were inveterate sun-worshippers, whereas Auden, with his alarming pallor (he claimed Icelandic descent), spent his days indoors working on *The Orators* (1932) while his friends frolicked on the beach. It was in Sellin that Spender took what he deprecatingly referred to as 'the most famous photograph in the history of the world' with his 'masturbatory camera designed for narcissists', which had a timer that allowed him to pose with his friends. 'Stephen', writes Isherwood, 'has his arms around Wystan and Christopher and an expression on his face which suggests an off-duty Jesus relaxing with "these little ones." Christopher, compared with the others, is such a very little one that he looks as if he is standing in a hole' (*CK*, 84).⁸ In Sellin, Isherwood was tormented by jealousy as Walter blithely

The 'most famous photograph in the history of the world': W. H. Auden, Stephen Spender and Isherwood on Rügen Island in the summer of 1931.

flirted with the sun-kissed girls on the beach and danced with them at the casino in the evenings. He would use this experience for the 'On Ruegen Island' section of *Goodbye to Berlin*, where the character of Peter Wilkinson is deputed to suffer the humiliations of his author with Otto Nowak, while Herr Issyvoo is given the dispassionate observer role of Spender and Auden.

The Memorial was published in February 1932. It received a few good reviews but this didn't translate into sales, and the book lost money for the Hogarth Press. The anonymous reviewer in the *Times Literary Supplement* (*TLS*) praised the 'three-dimensional completeness' of Isherwood's characters, and found the relationship between Eric and Lily particularly 'sensitive' and affecting.[9] Another reviewer balked at 'the disproportionately large number of homosexual characters' in the novel (*CK*, 91). Some of Isherwood's relatives also objected to the book, and were embarrassed by the parallels between Marple Hall and the Hall, Marple and Chapel Bridge, Frank Isherwood and Richard Vernon. They were particularly upset by Isherwood's portrait of John Vernon, the drooling owner of the Hall, finding it 'in the worst possible taste'. As for Kathleen, she had 'far more reason to dislike the novel but she never once complained that it had hurt her feelings', writes Isherwood. 'Indeed she became highly indignant when some critics gave it bad notices' (*KF*, 264).

The following month Turville-Petre asked Isherwood to join him for an extended spell in the small German border town of Mohrin (now Moryń and part of Poland), where they could enjoy a healthier lifestyle and get some work done. The idea appealed to Isherwood, who was now working on *Lions and Shadows*, but what clinched the deal was the young factotum whom Turville-Petre engaged, named Heinz Neddermeyer. Heinz was 'about seventeen' with fat lips and curly hair; he had been raised by his grandmother, and doubtless regarded Isherwood as a father figure, though Isherwood characterized his role as protective 'elder brother'. Unlike the narcissistic, work-shy Walter, 'Heinz actually enjoyed work for work's sake,' writes Isherwood. 'No lover, however literary, could have shared Christopher's work with him. But Heinz did the next best thing; while Christopher wrote, Heinz collaborated with him indirectly by sweeping the floors, tidying up the garden, cooking the meals' (*CK*, 95).

Isherwood spent August and September 1932 with Kathleen at 19 Pembroke Gardens, a rented semi-detached house on the south side of Kensington High Street. Jean Ross, who had now left Berlin for good, was living nearby in a Notting Hill hotel. He also caught up with Edward Upward, who had joined the Communist Party after undertaking a tour of the Soviet Union in April 1932.[10] Isherwood made some important new contacts during this London stay, such as John Lehmann, the critic and manager of the Hogarth Press, who had been instrumental in getting *The Memorial* published after it was rejected by Jonathan Cape. He was also introduced to his literary idol E. M. Forster, who had admired *The Memorial*. The meeting with Forster was felicitous and led to a rewarding correspondence, with Isherwood leavening his anecdotes of 'the boy world' in Berlin with reports on the political situation. In the general election of July

1932 the Nazis had garnered over 13 million votes and were now the largest party in the Reichstag. Perhaps feeling that his autobiography was frivolous in comparison, Isherwood set it aside and began work on *The Lost*, focusing on Ross's misadventures and his time with the Wolff family (the Nowaks in *Goodbye to Berlin*) in the Simeonstrasse. He dictated this partial draft to his brother Richard, who wrote it out in longhand.

Now that Isherwood was writing about his Berlin experiences, he began to perceive Spender as a threat. When he shared his best Berlin anecdotes with his London friends, he was chagrined to learn that they had already heard of Jean Ross and Gerald Hamilton from Spender. In an intemperate letter, he reproached Spender for being a literary interloper who was stealing his material, and vowed to live elsewhere if Spender remained in Berlin.[11] Spender was mortified but ceded the city to Isherwood, who, having asserted his will, attempted to repair the rift. In a letter from the 'Berlin battlefield', he wrote: 'I get uglier and more shrivelled every day. My hair is scurfy and drops out, my teeth are bad, my breath smells. However, I do see that it's absolutely necessary for me to stay on here at present.'[12] He boasted that he had been doing some translation work for the IAH (Internationale Arbeiter-Hilfe), an organization that provided famine relief to the Soviet Union, and affirmed that he was thinking about joining it as a token of his communist sympathies – but he never did, and, as he later admitted, this was the closest he came to being a communist.

Isherwood was bearing witness to the last days of the Weimar Republic. During the general strike of November 1932, he saw a group of zealous Nazis set about a young man, stabbing him with the points of their banners. 'The youth was such a clot of blood', he wrote to Spender, that he 'couldn't see how badly he was hurt, but I think one of the spikes had gone into his eye'.[13] This scene would later be fictionalized in *Goodbye to Berlin*, in which the youth's 'left eye was poked half out' (*GB*, 198). Despite having lost 2 million votes and 34 seats in the general election of November 1932, Hitler was appointed chancellor when the head of the cabinet, Kurt von Schleicher, resigned in January 1933. A month later, on 27 February,

Heinz Neddermeyer and Isherwood, *c.* mid-1930s.

the Reichstag was set on fire. Hitler asserted that the fire was evidence of a failed communist uprising and used the resulting state of emergency to invoke Article 48 of the Weimar constitution, which abrogated civil liberties, such as freedom of speech and freedom of association. This allowed the Nazi government to suppress the communists and their political enemies. In the general election of 5 March, Hitler and his allies won a majority in the Reichstag and facilitated the passage of the Enabling Act, which conferred on Hitler the powers of a dictator and inaugurated a new era: the Third Reich.

Following the general election, Nollendorfstrasse was festooned with swastikas, less from Nazi enthusiasm than because it was potentially dangerous not to advertise one's allegiance. When the boycott of Jewish businesses occurred on 1 April, Isherwood made a 'token purchase' from the department store owned by the family of Wilfred Israel, a Jewish friend who inspired the character of Bernhard Landauer in *Goodbye to Berlin*. He noted that one of the stormtroopers posted outside the store was a boy he knew from the Cosy Corner. The gay and lesbian bars that had been so intimately associated with the Weimar Republic were now being shut down. Magnus Hirschfeld had fled to France some years earlier, and his Institut für Sexualwissenschaft was raided in May by a posse of physical education students. They loaded trucks with books and papers from the archives, which were publicly burnt a few days later in the square before the opera house, along with other 'degenerate' books from Berlin libraries and a bust of Hirschfeld. Isherwood was present at the book burning and quietly spoke the word 'shame'.

He returned to London in early April and deposited his books and manuscripts with Kathleen at Pembroke Gardens. During this stay, he learned that three Englishmen had been arrested in Berlin, possibly for homosexuality, and Frl. Thurau reported that the police had visited her apartment to make enquiries about him due to his association with the 'Hirschfeld Homosexuals and the Hamilton Reds' (CK, 128). As a British citizen, the only real risk he ran was expulsion, but he was worried about Heinz, who was proving to be a more congenial partner than Walter. 'In the old days,' he wrote to Spender, 'I was obsessed with the idea of a *high tension!*, *extreme danger!* relationship, which gave off ten-foot sparks and electrocuted everyone in the neighborhood. Now I see that there's something to be said for decency and a little mutual consideration and pleasantness' (*CK*, 114).

Isherwood decided to accept Turville-Petre's invitation to stay on the tiny Greek island of St Nicholas (now called Ktiponisi). There was a tumulus on St Nicholas rumoured to contain prehistoric artefacts, and Turville-Petre had been able to lease the island for £3 a year. Isherwood made a final trip to Berlin at the end of April and departed for good on 13 May 1933 with Heinz and Erwin Hansen (the former caretaker of the Hirschfeld institute). They travelled through Europe by train and steamer and arrived in Athens a week later. St Nicholas was less than 1 kilometre long and was located about 300 metres from mainland Greece, in the North Euboean Gulf. The island was beautiful, with turquoise bays and pine-strewn hills, but there were no amenities. Turville-Petre was having a house constructed by incompetent builders, and the only accommodation was a couple of crude huts fashioned from branches and covered with a groundsheet. The drinking water was ferried to the island in benzine cans, which lent it a brackish taste, and, in conjunction with a diet of rank fish and retsina, caused Isherwood's ulcerative colitis to flare up. The kitchen (a roofless hut) was infested with flies. Isherwood was horrified when he spotted Petro (one of the ragtag group of boys who camped on the island) washing up without water by wiping the dirty dishes on a cloth another boy had worn round his head. To make matters worse, Petro had both syphilis and gonorrhoea, and his skin was filthy with sores.[14]

Even after Isherwood had purchased a tent for himself and Heinz, in which he installed a table for his typewriter, he found it impossible to concentrate, what with the commotion of the builders and the malicious boys who played gramophone records while he was trying to write. Instead of making progress on *The Lost*, he found himself making querulous entries in his diary that he was hoping to turn into a lucrative travel book, but while this never came to pass it did serve as the raw material for the 'Ambrose' section of *Down There on a Visit*. Another distraction was Heinz, who enjoyed the builders' company, while Isherwood, for all his pretensions to solidarity with the workers, regarded the Greeks as 'dagoes – the swine of the earth'.[15] Heinz also fraternized with 'the boys', who were all sexually insatiable and apparently had no qualms about bestiality (Isherwood mentions in passing that one of the boys 'raped a duck'). He confessed to being 'jealous of everyone on the island' and this destabilized his relationship with Heinz (*CK*, 146).

By the beginning of September Isherwood had had enough of island life and picked a fight with Heinz as a pretext for splitting up. The plan had been to put Heinz on a train to Berlin, but there were no sleeping berths available, so Isherwood reluctantly took him on the steamer to Marseille, vowing to dump him in Paris. Away from the tensions of the island, though, they were quickly reconciled, and spent a couple of weeks in Meudon (on the outskirts of Paris) visiting Isherwood's communist friend Rolf Katz. In London, Isherwood introduced Heinz to his mother. While perfectly polite, Kathleen treated Heinz as a social inferior, but this wasn't simple snobbery: her attitude to Heinz was doubtless coloured by her son's toxic relationship with Walter (another working-class German boy). There was also the delicate matter of his nationality, and the fact that Kathleen's husband had been killed by Germans in the war. When Heinz's visa expired in the middle of October, he was forced to return to Berlin, but Isherwood was determined to bring him back.

Meanwhile, Jean Ross had recommended Isherwood to the Austrian film director Berthold Viertel, who was looking for someone to write a screen adaptation of *Little Friend* by Ernst Lothar, which turns on a girl whose failed suicide reunites her warring parents. On the strength of reading the botched suicide of Edward Blake in *The Memorial*, Viertel gave Isherwood the job. Viertel had been a theatre director in Berlin, where he made the transition to film. He moved to Hollywood in 1928 following financial setbacks, but was disillusioned with the commercial films the studios wanted him to make, and had come to England in search of more artistic projects. In *Lions and Shadows*, Isherwood describes himself as a 'born film fan' and frames his cinematic obsession in literary terms: for someone who is 'endlessly interested in the outward appearance of people', the cinema allows one to study 'their facial expressions, their gestures, their walk', as if 'under a microscope' (*LS*, 60). Thus the opportunity of learning film-making from a master like Viertel was irresistible, and the salary of £125 a week (£7,400 today) was a bonus.[16] Viertel liked to expatiate on art and women, and mortified Isherwood by making homophobic jokes. But as with Gerald Hamilton and Jean Ross, Isherwood was aware that here was another literary character in the making, and he would use his experience of making *Little Friend* with Viertel when he sat down to write *Prater Violet* in 1943.

While working on the screenplay with Viertel, Isherwood was asked to be dialogue director during the shoot, which would mean another two months in London. Wanting Heinz to join him, he sent him some money to prove he wasn't in the country to work, and dictated a letter to Kathleen, in which she invited Heinz to stay with her in Pembroke Gardens. Heinz's boat arrived in Harwich on 5 January 1934. Isherwood travelled down with Auden to meet him and endured a humiliating interview with the immigration officials. Heinz had mistakenly showed them the letter from Isherwood in which he instructed Heinz to pretend that the money he enclosed was from his grandmother. The officials asked Isherwood why Kathleen would want to entertain a domestic servant from Germany, insinuated that Heinz was Isherwood's 'sweetheart' and, unmoved by Isherwood's patrician bluster, deported Heinz to Germany. The scheme had been scuppered, Auden perceived, because one of the officials was gay: 'As soon as I saw that bright-eyed little rat, I knew we were done for,' he exclaimed. 'He understood the whole situation at a glance – because he's *one of us*' (*CK*, 166).

Before starting the shoot, Isherwood met up with Heinz in Amsterdam and arranged for him to stay with a family there and learn English. Back in London, Isherwood studied the film-making process with fascination. He quizzed the electricians, carpenters and cameramen about their jobs and delighted in the technical jargon. The studio was in Lime Grove, Shepherd's Bush, and Isherwood would run into film-makers and actors in the Goldhawk pub. He invited literary friends, including Forster, to the set, and let them assume that he was now tremendously wealthy, making a big show of paying for their meals and taxis. Much as Isherwood relished his new role, he abandoned the shoot before it was finished to join Heinz in Amsterdam at the end of March.

He was also eager to resume work on *The Lost*, but rereading what he'd written he perceived that his original plan was unfeasible. *The Lost* had combined the characters of *Mr Norris Changes Trains* and *Goodbye to Berlin*, imposed on them a semblance of plot and relied on coincidence and unlikely connections to draw them together. Each character had been intended to exemplify an aspect of the lost: lost in the sense of being led astray by Nazi propaganda (for example Frl. Schroeder at the end of *Mr Norris*); lost as in danger of being killed by the Nazis (like Bernhard Landauer in *Goodbye to Berlin*); or lost as in beyond the pale in polite society (Sally Bowles and Arthur Norris). But while Isherwood's ambition was epic, in practice he was unable to orchestrate such a large cast of characters, and chose to concentrate on Arthur Norris instead. He and Heinz had moved to Tenerife in June, and writing in the garden of their pension in La Orotava he completed *Mr Norris Changes Trains* in two months.

The novel signalled a new direction in Isherwood's work. It was narrated in the first person by William Bradshaw (Isherwood's middle names). The choice of a first-person narrator was a hangover from *The Lost*: he felt that as an outsider he couldn't pretend to know his German characters from the inside, as he'd done with the English cast of *The Memorial*, conveying their personalities through interior monologues.[17] Furthermore, with a mysterious character like Arthur Norris, third-person interiority would spoil the surprise of his schemes and smokescreens, which must be perceived from without. Isherwood had intended to write what he called a 'dynamic portrait' of Norris, in the manner of the character sketches of *Goodbye to Berlin*, but under the influence of working with Viertel on *Little Friend*, he produced a 'constructed' novel instead, with an espionage plot that he later regretted.[18]

Despite the significance of his name, William Bradshaw is no more autobiographical than Philip Lindsay or Eric Vernon. Critics often assume that Bradshaw is a writer, but all we know for sure is that he lives in Berlin and supports himself by giving English lessons. Unlike Lindsay, who talks endlessly about his artistic projects, Bradshaw never mentions writing and seems devoid of ambition. As with Lindsay and Vernon, a discreet veil has been drawn over Bradshaw's sexuality. There were several reasons for this: first, he didn't want to embarrass Kathleen and feared that Uncle Henry might rescind his allowance if he tarnished the Isherwood name; second, he wanted the reader to identify with Bradshaw, and felt that making Bradshaw openly homosexual would prevent this; and third, he wanted the focus of the novel to be Norris and feared that depicting Bradshaw's sex life would be a distraction.[19] Consequently, Bradshaw appears almost as mysterious as Norris and we never learn, for example, why he has chosen to live in Berlin. One of Bradshaw's virtues as a narrator is his non-judgemental attitude to other people's sexual predilections. For instance, when he discovers the middle-aged Norris in his 'mauve silk underwear' being whipped by two women at a New Year's Eve party, he describes the scene with admirable sangfroid (*MNCT*, 36). Likewise, when Norris's friend, the Baron von Pregnitz, shares with Bradshaw his fantasy of living on one of the Pacific Islands with a stable of adolescent boys, and lends him the young adult book on which it is based, Bradshaw reads it without demur. He also reads most of Norris's collection of BDSM novels, and expresses his fondness for *Miss Smith's Torture Chamber*, which Norris reveals was written by himself.[20]

Bradshaw meets Norris on a train to Berlin and is charmed by his courtly manners, rather obvious wig and *fin-de-siècle* aestheticism. In many ways, Bradshaw is as much of a fantasist as Norris and the Baron; he spins a romantic web around Norris that he knows is false: 'I wanted to imagine [Norris] as a glorified being; audacious and self-reliant, reckless and calm. All of which, in reality, he only too painfully and obviously wasn't' (*MNCT*, 43). Bradshaw takes an immediate dislike to Norris's 'secretary' Schmidt, but fails to perceive that he is a necessary counterpart to Norris's dandy, a hardnosed brute who will transact the dirty business of his master.[21]

It transpires that Norris has spent eighteen months in prison for blackmail, but his winning orotundity aestheticizes the crime: 'I do and always shall maintain that it is the privilege of the richer but less mentally endowed members of the community to contribute to the upkeep of people like myself' (*MNCT*, 47).

The chief theme of the novel is the interpenetration of the private and the public, the personal and the political. This is symbolized when Bradshaw visits Norris for the first time and realizes that the two doors of his residence – one marked 'Arthur Norris. Private' and the other 'Arthur Norris. Export and Import' – are only separated by a curtain (*MNCT*, 15).[22] As a result of his profligacy, Norris is importuned by creditors and becomes involved with the Communist Party in order to sell their secrets to a French agent. Bradshaw goes to a communist meeting to hear Norris deploy his rhetorical gifts against British imperialism in East Asia. Like his creator, Bradshaw is drawn to the communist *esprit de corps* but is chary of political commitment; like Isherwood, he agrees to do some translation work for the party. But the communist leader Ludwig Bayer is a cold-eyed realist who sees Norris for what he is, and uses him to pass disinformation to the enemy.

The narrative unfolds over the period 1930–33 and is punctuated by Bradshaw's reports on the Nazi ascendancy:

> Berlin was in a state of civil war. Hate exploded suddenly, without warning, out of nowhere; at street corners, in restaurants, cinemas, dance halls, swimming-baths ... Knives were whipped out, blows were dealt with spiked rings, beer-mugs, chair-legs, or leaded clubs; bullets slashed the advertisements on the poster-columns, rebounded from the iron roofs of latrines. (*MNCT*, 104)

Bradshaw's personal relations with Norris have political repercussions. The Baron is an official in the German government and Norris tricks Bradshaw into inviting the Baron to a Swiss ski resort, where 'Margot' (the French agent) will be waiting, telling Bradshaw that 'Margot' is a businessman who wants to strike a deal with the Baron. Bradshaw is disabused by Bayer, who recalls him from

Switzerland and informs him that the police are aware of Norris's activities. When Norris flees the country, his secretary Schmidt starts blackmailing the Baron (he has some incriminating letters the Baron sent to a minor), who commits suicide. And the communist Bayer is murdered in the aftermath of the Nazi usurpation of power.

In his introduction to Gerald Hamilton's book *Mr Norris and I*, Isherwood judged *Mr Norris Changes Trains* 'a heartless fairy-story about a real city in which human beings were suffering the miseries of political violence and near-starvation'. He maintained he was attracted by the reputation of Berlin as a modern-day Sodom and was in search of 'civil monsters' (the phrase is from *Othello*), but the 'only genuine monster was the young foreigner who passed gaily through these scenes of desolation, misinterpreting them to suit his childish fantasy'.[23] While there is perhaps a germ of truth in this charge, it seems too harsh. Far from the narrative of *Mr Norris* being grafted onto the political conflict of Weimar Berlin for local colour, Isherwood creates telling parallels between Norris and Hitler that serve to domesticate the tragedy. As Claude Summers has noted, Norris's 'sadomasochistic pleasures parody the real sadism of the Nazi regime', while Norris's intrigues parody the political machinations of Hitler. And the reader's indulgent affection for Norris 'becomes analogous to the average German's political enthusiasm for Hitler'.[24] In a letter from Mexico, Norris describes the Nazis as 'nothing more or less than *criminals*' and affirms: 'It is indeed tragic to see how, even in these days, a *clever* and *unscrupulous liar* can deceive millions' (MNCT, 227–8; italics in original). 'The effect of the book's irony', writes Summers, 'is not only to condemn [Bradshaw's] naivety and passivity but also to force the reader toward compassionate understanding, both for [Bradshaw] and for the German people.'[25]

Mr Norris Changes Trains was published in February 1935 and garnered good reviews. William Plomer, writing in *The Spectator*, judged *Mr Norris* 'continuously amusing and intelligent from the first page to the last'.[26] Gerald Hamilton, who initially withheld his permission to publish the book on the grounds that he would never betray the Communist Party, was now delighted with his alter ego.

'He eagerly searches the press for reviews', Isherwood informed his mother, 'and notes successes with proprietary pride: "We got a very good notice in the Telegraph," etc!'[27] On the other hand, Uncle Henry deplored the book for sullying the Bradshaw name by associating it with characters of dubious repute, causing Isherwood to worry about the next payment of his allowance.

Due to Heinz's nationality, Isherwood was forced to lead a nomadic existence, and for the next few years he and Heinz moved restlessly around Europe – Copenhagen, Brussels, Amsterdam, Portugal, Paris – their fate dictated by immigration officials and temporary residence permits. In March 1935 Hitler defied the Treaty of Versailles and announced the introduction of conscription, which meant that it was only a matter of time before Heinz was issued with conscription papers; if he didn't return to Germany, he would be deprived of German citizenship and expelled from whatever country he was in. This prompted Isherwood to look for a more permanent solution, and so when Gerald Hamilton offered to procure Heinz a new nationality for £1,000 (almost £60,000 today) he eventually accepted. Inevitably, Isherwood asked Kathleen for the money, who expressed profound reservations with the plan, but ultimately she capitulated to her son's demand.

Isherwood began writing the first chapter of what would become *Lions and Shadows* in the autumn of 1936, and asked Kathleen to send him papers and diaries from his time at Repton. In light of the Spanish Civil War that had erupted in July, Isherwood worried that his 'reminiscences of the twenties [would] seem like the chatter of a nursery governess over the tea-table'.[28] Auden resolved to help the Republicans, either as an ambulance driver or as a soldier. Although he occasionally adopted Marxist attitudes, Isherwood affirmed that at heart Auden was a Christian. In his recent collaborations with Isherwood – the idiosyncratic anti-fascist plays *The Dog Beneath the Skin* (1935) and *The Ascent of F6* (1936) – Auden had attacked the ivory-tower artist; in a letter to a family friend explaining his reasons for going to Spain, he lamented that 'I can speak with authority about la Condition Humaine of only a small class of English intellectuals,' and he hoped that participating in the war would make him a more inclusive poet.²⁹ 'I can't help feeling the worst sort of swine to be staying safe here when Wystan is going,' Isherwood wrote to Spender. 'And yet I can't leave H. in the middle of his passport business being arranged, and I do want to finish my book.'³⁰ In Valencia, however, the officials decided that Auden could more profitably pursue a propaganda role, and he made some ineffectual radio broadcasts. After briefly witnessing the fighting at first hand in Sariñena, he returned to England on 4 March, having been in Spain less than two months.³¹

On a visit to London in April 1937, Isherwood learned that Heinz had been arrested after a drunken fracas with the police in Paris and was being expelled from France. Isherwood was currently bedridden with an ulcerated mouth after a botched dental extraction, and had to send an American admirer named Tony Bower to escort Heinz to Luxembourg. Isherwood arrived a week later and consulted with Cecil Salinger, the lawyer Hamilton had entrusted to obtain a Mexican passport for Heinz. They had by then been waiting for several months, and the passport still hadn't arrived when, on 12 May, two policemen turned up at their hotel to inform them that Heinz was being expelled from Luxembourg and had six hours to leave. According to Salinger, the French authorities had passed on their list of 'undesirables' to their Luxembourg counterparts. Salinger promised to obtain an emergency Belgian visa for Heinz, but with nowhere else to go, Heinz was forced to return to Germany, where he was arrested by the Gestapo. Salinger engaged a German lawyer to defend Heinz and travelled to Brussels, where Isherwood was waiting, to break the news. The German lawyer advised Heinz to pretend that he had been seduced by a degenerate foreigner who was addicted to 'reciprocal onanism' (from the Nazi point of view, this was the least obnoxious homosexual act), and had been dragged round Europe to service his desire. Isherwood agreed to this defence and Heinz was given a sentence of six months in prison and one year of labour service to the state, followed by two years in the army.

In the aftermath, Isherwood was both devastated and, though he could only admit to this later, relieved. On the one hand, four years of constant travelling with Heinz and visa negotiations had been extremely stressful; on the other, saving Heinz from the Nazis had lent purpose to his life and he was left contemplating the void. In his diary, he noted: 'To those who find themselves in a situation like mine, I can't recommend masturbation too highly. Judiciously practised, it dulls your feelings almost completely. Only, if you do it too much, you feel more miserable than ever.'[32] He grew suspicious about Gerald Hamilton's involvement and wondered whether he hadn't conspired to have Heinz deported in order not to have to produce the Mexican passport that had, according to Salinger, belatedly arrived. To stop himself brooding about Heinz, Isherwood hunkered down in his Brussels hotel and finished a first draft of *Lions and Shadows* before returning to London on 21 June.

He had also been working on the *disjecta membra* of *The Lost*. John Lehmann had asked him to contribute to his periodical *New Writing* and Isherwood gave him 'The Nowaks', which was published to considerable acclaim in the spring of 1936. The proletarian realism of 'The Nowaks' went over well with Isherwood's left-leaning friends. He also wrote 'Berlin Diary' at this time, but he hadn't yet hit on the idea of these fragments comprising the novel *Goodbye to Berlin*. He had planned to publish 'Sally Bowles' in *New Writing*, too, but Lehmann objected to its length and wanted Isherwood to excise Sally's illegal abortion, which Isherwood refused to do. In the end, Isherwood gave him 'Berlin Diary' instead and published *Sally Bowles* (1937) as a stand-alone novella with the Hogarth Press.[33]

Isherwood finished *Lions and Shadows* in September. It is his first book that can properly be described as autofiction. In his prefatory note to the reader, he writes: 'I had better start by saying what this book is not: it is not, in the ordinary journalistic sense of the word, an autobiography; it contains no "revelations"; it is never "indiscreet"; it is not even entirely "true."' His previous book, *Mr Norris Changes Trains*, comes close to being an autofiction, but finally feels more akin to an autobiographical novel, albeit one in which the narrator shares the author's middle names. In *Lions and Shadows*, while Isherwood appears to be writing an autobiography, he disavows the category and claims that the events depicted in it are not wholly true. 'Read it as a novel,' he writes. 'I have used a novelist's licence in describing my incidents and drawing my characters: "Chalmers," "Linsley," "Cheuret" and "Weston" are all caricatures: that is why . . . I have given them, and nearly everybody else, fictitious names' (*LS*, n.p.).

It's significant that he chose the *nom de guerre* Chalmers for Edward Upward, since this is the name he had given the Upward character in his first novel *All the Conspirators*. But in the latter Chalmers shared certain details with Hector Wintle, such as being a medical student, whereas in *Lions and Shadows* Chalmers is a history scholar at Cambridge. Moreover, in *All the Conspirators* the protagonist Philip Lindsay shared certain details with Isherwood and Wintle, but in *Lions and Shadows* Wintle is given the name Philip Linsley, and would have appeared there as Philip Lindsay had it not been for an officious lawyer at the Hogarth Press who worried that the real-life author Philip Lindsay would object. This intertextuality was readily embraced by Isherwood's friends. For example, in Spender's autobiography *World within World* he uses the name Allen Chalmers to write about Upward. When Upward belatedly published the longest Mortmere story, 'The Railway Accident', in 1949, he did so under the pseudonym Allen Chalmers.[34] And when, much later, Upward came to fictionalize his experiences at Repton and Cambridge in *No Home but the Struggle*, he borrowed Isherwood's *noms de guerre* for the history master at Repton (Mr Holmes) and the history don at Cambridge (Gorse) from *Lions and Shadows*, and used the name Rugtonstead (an amalgam of Rugby, Repton, Berkhamsted and Eton) as a fictional analogue for Repton, which first appeared in Isherwood's apprentice novels.[35]

This liberal intermingling of fiction and autobiography, which would become a hallmark of Isherwood's work, is unsurprising when one considers that he had first conceived of the book around the time he was working on *The Lost*, which was envisaged as pressing factual material into a fictional plot; however, he had abandoned this idea and had published some of the material as fictional fragments of the Berlin diary of 'Christopher Isherwood'. While these fragments would appear in the novel *Goodbye to Berlin*, he had at one point thought about including them in a sprawling autobiography that would incorporate the material Isherwood used in *Lions and Shadows*. Furthermore, the book is structured along the same lines as *Goodbye to Berlin* as a series of 'dynamic portraits', including his history master from Repton, Edward Upward, Hector Wintle, the Mangeots, Auden. And while the narrator of *Lions and Shadows* is less self-effacing than the 'Isherwood' of *Goodbye to Berlin*, he attempts to bring a camera-like objectivity to his younger self. 'I try to be very objective and as far as possible impersonal,' he wrote to Spender while working on the book, 'just speaking for my epoch, class, income, nationality, background, etc. . . . I am at present writing the book with assumed names for Edward, Wystan and my friends, because it seems so much easier to write objectively if you don't use real ones.'[36]

In *Lions and Shadows*, Isherwood presents a comic portrait of the artist as a young man, with all his early work and embarrassing juvenilia, such as the Mortmere stories, laid bare for scrutiny. But where Joyce, in his novel *A Portrait of the Artist as a Young Man* (1916), is all high artistic seriousness, with his autobiographical protagonist vowing to 'forge in the smithy of my soul the uncreated conscience of my race', Isherwood's book is about artistic failure and at the end he departs for Germany to sever the apron strings of mummy and nanny and take his first faltering steps towards adulthood.[37] For critics, *Lions and Shadows* has been a seminal text, for here Isherwood unveils his personal mythos, with its archetypes (the others, the watcher in Spanish, the truly weak and the truly strong man), a private language (quisb,[38] the test, tea-tabling), heroes such as Chalmers and Weston and villains (Laily, the poshocracy). This mythos provides a key to unlock the obscurities of his earlier work (and some of Auden's poetry), but there's a danger in cleaving to it unquestioningly. For example, one of the archetypes of the Isherwood mythos is the demon-mother, and several critics, most notably Cyril Connolly, have described Mrs Lindsay in *All the Conspirators* as a demonic or 'evil mother', which is hyperbolic at best, misleading at worse, for Mrs Lindsay is selfish, yes, and manipulative, but, as Colin Wilson notes, 'scarcely evil'.[39]

Much of the book's considerable charm derives from Isherwood's seemingly unabashed (though perhaps calculating) candour in confessing to bad behaviour. The suggestion is that *of course* he behaved hypocritically, for example by courting the attentions of the poshocracy while vilifying them to Chalmers and pretending to be a spy; *of course* he did nothing but sit and stupidly smile when the poshocracy started a butter fight in Chalmers's rooms, which left butter everywhere and led Chalmers to the brink of ending their friendship. Despite Isherwood's contention that his portraits of his friends are mere caricatures, they are evoked as artfully as Sally Bowles and Mr Norris. For instance, here he is on Weston (Auden):

> He smoked enormously, insatiably: 'Insufficient weaning,' he explained. 'I must have something to suck.' And he drank more cups of tea per day than anybody else I have ever known. It was as if his large, white apparently bloodless body needed continual reinforcements of warmth. Although this was the height of the summer, he insisted, if the day was cloudy, on having a fire in the sitting-room. At night he slept with two thick blankets, an eiderdown, both our overcoats and all the rugs in his bedroom piled upon his bed. (*LS*, 145)

Weston et al. are caricatures only insofar as they lack the inexhaustible depth of the real people they represent.

Isherwood's musings about the test of war, and the surrogate tests he undertakes to prove his manhood, such as riding a motorbike, are lent urgency by the fact that in 1937 he was nervously anticipating another European war and wondering how he would react. Indeed, much of what he writes about the test seems as germane to himself in 1937 as it did in the 1920s:

> Isherwood the artist . . . stood apart from and above 'The Test' – because the Test was something for the common herd, it applied only to the world of everyday life. Isherwood refused the Test – not out of weakness, not out of cowardice, but because he was

subjected, daily, hourly, to a 'Test' of his own: the self-imposed Test of his integrity as a writer. (*LS*, 69)

Although Isherwood skewers the pretentions of his erstwhile aestheticism in *Lions and Shadows*, it should not be supposed that he no longer nurtured artistic pretensions that (in his own mind, at any rate) elevated him above the hoi polloi. Moreover, as will be seen in the next chapter, Isherwood and Auden spurned the test of the Second World War by emigrating to America.

4
Ivar Avenue, 1938–44

In the summer of 1937 Faber & Faber had asked Isherwood and Auden to write a travel book, and they settled on China. Animosity between China and Japan had been building since the Japanese invasion of Manchuria in 1931 and the establishment of the Japanese puppet state of Manchukuo in 1932. The Marco Polo Bridge Incident on 7 July 1937, in which gunfire was exchanged between Chinese and Japanese soldiers, marked the unofficial start of the Second Sino-Japanese War (1937–45) and led to the Japanese annexation of Beijing and Shanghai later that year. Where the Spanish Civil War was attracting literary legends such as Ernest Hemingway and André Malraux, no one of any note was reporting on China. In preparation, Isherwood put the finishing touches to the diary fragments and portraits that comprised *Goodbye to Berlin* and left the manuscript with John Lehmann in case he was killed in China. A considerable fanfare accompanied their departure, and on 19 January 1938 the press assembled at Victoria Station, where a historic photo of the writers was taken in front of the smoking carriage of the Dover train, with the two friends gamely grinning in the limelight.

Wherever they went in China, Isherwood and Auden were treated like celebrities: at Guangdong, they met the British consul-general; in Wuchang they met Chiang Kai-shek and his wife. They experienced their first air raid in Wuhan: after climbing to the roof of a high building with the consul, they spotted six Japanese planes illuminated by searchlights. In the travel diary he shared with Auden, Isherwood depicted the Japanese in pathological terms: 'It was as if a microscope had brought dramatically into focus the bacilli of a fatal disease. They passed, bright, tiny, and deadly, infecting the night.'[1]

At the end of March, they stoically set out for the front in four rickshaws: one for their servant Chiang, one for their luggage (which included folding camp beds and linen) and two for themselves. The road proved to be so bad, though, that they had to walk some of the way. Isherwood was vainly attired in his war reporter's costume – 'beret, sweater, and martial boots [that] would not be out of place in Valencia or Madrid' – and was envious of Auden's 'rubber shoes' as his boots were giving him blisters.[2] They had to petition a general for permission to approach the front on the banks of the Grand Canal, and were accompanied by officers to defensive lines miles from the actual fighting lest they come to harm. It was only after much cajolery that the officers agreed to take them to Hanzhuang village, where the Japanese troops were billeted during the day, but this proved anticlimactic.[3] After sticking his head above the parapet and taking some photos, Auden cheerfully announced: 'I don't believe . . . that there are any Japs here at all.'[4] Presently, the Chinese commenced an artillery bombardment, and Isherwood and Auden were forced to retreat. Once in the open, they had to dive for cover in the fields to avoid being spotted by the Japanese aircraft overhead, which were searching for the heavy Chinese guns.

In May they made another attempt to witness the fighting with the adventurer Peter Fleming, a special correspondent for *The Times*. Initially, they resented Fleming for being a proper war reporter but finally succumbed to his swashbuckling charm and agreed to travel with him to a dangerous front near Taihu Lake. After a gruelling five-day trek, though, they were forced to retreat the way they had come. By this time, Isherwood and Auden were so exhausted they allowed the 'coolies' to carry them in chairs.[5] This was their last attempt at war reporting; they took a steamer boat to Shanghai, arriving on 25 May. Here they stayed at the British ambassador's residence and took 'holidays from their social consciences' in the bathhouses, which offered erotic massage (*CK*, 318).

Isherwood and W. H. Auden setting off for China at Victoria Station, 19 January 1938.

During their travels, Isherwood's relationship with Auden had become frayed. 'In China I sometimes found myself really hating him,' Isherwood wrote in his diary. 'I was meanly jealous of him, too. Jealous of his share of the limelight; jealous because he'll no longer play the role of dependent, admiring younger brother. Indeed, I got such a *physical* dislike of him that I deliberately willed him to get ill; which he did.'[6]

Peter Parker suggests that Isherwood wanted Auden to get sick (they both got dysentery) so that he wouldn't have to sleep with him, and that this signalled the end of their sexual relationship, which had endured for over a decade.[7] To make matters worse, when they arrived in New York the following month, Isherwood became infatuated with a blond all-American boy with 'very sexy legs' named Harvey Young.[8] The latter had just turned 17 whereas Auden, at the age of 31, was for Isherwood a bit long in the tooth. In New York and on the voyage back to England in July, Isherwood recalled the 'extraordinary scenes', with 'Wystan in tears, telling me that no one would ever love him, that he would never have my sexual success'.[9]

Their nine-day stay in New York was powered by the amphetamine Benzedrine. They had been sending travel pieces to George Davis, the fiction editor at *Harper's Bazaar*, who presented them with 'wads of dollar bills' on their arrival. Davis acted as a tour guide and introduced them to celebrities such as Orson Welles and the composer Kurt Weill. According to Auden, both he and Isherwood resolved during their time in New York to return and settle in the United States.[10] But Isherwood's attitude seems to have been more temporizing: 'In those days, Christopher's plans were all provisional. If he had had someone to stay in England for, he might never have gone to America' (*LY*, 106n). Moreover, his exposure to real danger in China through air raids and shelling had blunted his 'neurotic fear of "War" as a concept', and he was now confident that he wouldn't humiliate himself in a crisis (*CK*, 323). At some point that summer, while Hitler was threatening to invade Czechoslovakia, Isherwood and John Lehmann approached the Foreign Office to volunteer for propaganda work. But by the time the news broke of the Munich Agreement at the end of September, Isherwood had already made up his mind: 'That doesn't matter any more to me,' he told Lehmann. 'I shall be in America.'[11]

Indeed, while officially disgusted with Chamberlain's pusillanimous diplomacy, he was secretly relieved that war had been postponed, since he wanted to finish writing his part of the travel book about China, *Journey to a War* (1939), before emigrating to America. In December Isherwood joined Auden in Brussels to hammer out a finished draft. The book comprises photographs, poems and a sonnet sequence by Auden, and a 'travel-diary' by Isherwood. While in Brussels, Isherwood also corrected the proofs of *Goodbye to Berlin* and contracted gonorrhoea from a male prostitute.[12] He briefly returned to London in January and had a tearful farewell with Kathleen, who had shocked him by turning seventy a few months previously (she always looked much younger than her age), and it struck him that he might not see her again. 'It was sad,' he writes, 'sad as dying, to leave these loved ones behind,' and yet as soon as the train pulled out of the station, he felt a surge of relief and exchanged a 'schoolboy grin' with Auden (CK, 343). Their ship sailed from Southampton on 19 January 1939, exactly a year after they had embarked together on their trip to China, which Isherwood inferred as a good omen.

In *Christopher and His Kind*, Isherwood proclaims during the crossing: 'You know, it just doesn't mean anything to me any more – the Popular Front, the party line, the anti-Fascist struggle . . . I simply cannot swallow another mouthful.' And Auden replies: 'Neither can I' (CK, 344). For some time, Auden had felt a cognitive dissonance between his private convictions and his public persona, which condemned fascism in lectures and deferred to the communist line in his collaborations with Isherwood.[13] As a Christian, Auden could hardly be expected to subscribe to dialectical materialism, which disavowed the existence of God and regarded religion as a comforting illusion. Furthermore, he had been appalled by the razing of churches and the anti-Catholic propaganda he had witnessed in Spain. For Isherwood, who was an atheist at this time, the problem was Heinz, with whom he was still corresponding and who was now undergoing the labour-service part of his sentence, which would be followed by two years in the army. Isherwood simply refused to fight against a German army that had Heinz in it and so he resolved to become a pacifist. In fact, musing about it in his diary, he claimed that he'd been a pacifist in all but name ever since he was a boy whose hatred of war was inspired by the example of his father and who despised the mindless patriotism that was de rigueur at his prep school.

Parker questions the 'self-mythologizing' patness of Isherwood's pacifist conversion en route to America.[14] Certainly, his letters from this time paint a less resolute picture. In February he wrote to Kathleen: 'There's no point in going to Hollywood if we have to come racing home again.'[15] It's not until the end of March that he reported: 'I think we are both rapidly becoming less political, and considerably more definitely pacifist.' He added: 'I still think, if war breaks out, that we shall come back; but only to share the suffering. Neither of us will fight.'[16] In contrast to their previous trip to New York, which had been a glamorous swirl of Benzedrine, sex and celebrities, New York in winter was a chastening experience. For the first few months he and Auden stayed at the George Washington Hotel in Gramercy Park. Here Isherwood tried to make some progress with a new novel but found himself unable to write.

In a letter to Kathleen in February, Isherwood mentioned in passing that Salinger (the lawyer he'd engaged to secure Heinz's naturalization papers) had been arrested in Belgium in connection with the case of a Jewish doctor named Frédéric Imianitoff.[17] The precise details of the case suggest that Hamilton and Salinger had cheated Isherwood out of the money he'd paid for Heinz's Mexican passport. At this time, Salinger and Hamilton were blackmailing Herbert Singer (the grandson of the founder of the Singer Company), having discovered from a private detective that he'd had sex with a minor.[18] Imianitoff had a position in the Belgian government and had falsely claimed to have served in the British army. Under pressure from political enemies to prove this, Imianitoff, who had somehow learned that Salinger was blackmailing Singer, coerced Salinger into forging demobilization papers for him. To aggravate matters, Hamilton then began to blackmail Imianitoff, but whereas Salinger and Imianitoff went to prison, Hamilton absconded. Isherwood learned of Salinger's arrest as he boarded the boat-train for Southampton, and some months later he reported to Kathleen: 'Salinger got 4½ years. I can't help feeling sorry, even if he was all we feared, and worse.'[19] But it seems Isherwood was ignorant of Hamilton's exact role in the case, for he continued to correspond with Hamilton, and in response to his death in 1970 he wrote in his diary: 'I don't give a damn whether or not he swindled us – though I would love to know, simply out of curiosity' (*D*3, 87).

Due to his writer's block, Isherwood was crushed by the indifferent American reception of *Goodbye to Berlin* when it was published in March, despite the strongly favourable reviews it had attracted in England. 'I wish I could write novels, real ones, but perhaps I can't,' he lamented to Kathleen. 'Maybe I have come to the limit of my talent, and shall just go on being "promising" until people are tired of me.'[20] By 'real novels' Isherwood may have been thinking of the tightly plotted 'entertainments' of his cousin Graham Greene; however, one of the strengths of *Goodbye to Berlin* was that he had dropped the cumbersome plot of *The Lost* in favour of a series of incisive character sketches. As he himself would later realize, when he had gained some objectivity, as a writer he was a portraitist rather than a landscape painter. Unable to give an encyclopaedic account of Berlin in the manner of Joyce's Dublin, or the Manhattan of John Dos Passos, Isherwood faithfully captures the mood of the city through its characters. The Nazi ascendancy, rather than taking centre stage, is tea-tabled to the margins. For instance, there is the unashamed antisemitism of Frl. Mayr, one of the lodgers in Frl. Schroeder's apartment, who sabotages the engagement of the 'Galician Jewess' in the flat below; the swastika flags on the beach of Rügen Island and the sinister Nazi doctor who tells the narrator that Otto is a 'bad degenerate type' who should be sent to a 'labour camp'; the SA men who savage a political opponent in the street, stabbing him in the eye with the point of a Nazi banner;[21] the casual way in which Frl. Schroeder begins 'reverently' to refer to 'Der Führer', having voted Communist in the previous election.

Among other things, *Goodbye to Berlin* is an exemplary work of autofiction. If his autobiography *Lions and Shadows* reads like a work of fiction (with its 'fictitious names' and 'novelist's licence'), his novel *Goodbye to Berlin* gives the appearance of artless autobiography (with its diary sections and namesake narrator). And where readers of his autobiography were instructed to read it 'as a novel', in the preface of his novel Isherwood warns the reader not to interpret the book as a straightforward autobiography. 'Because I have given my own name to the "I" of this narrative,' he writes, 'readers are certainly not entitled to assume that its pages are purely autobiographical, or that its characters are libellously exact portraits of living persons. "Christopher Isherwood" is a convenient ventriloquist's dummy, nothing more' (*GB*, 6).

In a lecture from 1963, Isherwood asserted that he'd found the William Bradshaw of *Mr Norris* 'unsatisfactory' and 'strange', and resolved to 'write with an "I" who would be as much me as possible'.[22] On the one hand, the namesake narrator of *Goodbye to Berlin* is slightly more autobiographical than Bradshaw, in that he is a writer whose first novel, *All the Conspirators*, was a flop. On the other hand, he's just as sexless and inscrutable as Bradshaw, and for the same reasons: not wanting to attract too much attention to the camera of 'Christopher Isherwood', through whose lens we see the characters; not wanting to alienate the reader by revealing his homosexuality. At one point, the narrator describes himself as 'very queer indeed' but in a context that makes it plausible that he is merely expressing solidarity with the cross-dressers inside the Salomé club; his heterosexual companion Fritz Wendel tells the tactless American tourist who wants to know whether the cabaret artistes are 'queer': 'Eventually we're all queer' (*GB*, 190).

The reader's sympathies are immediately engaged by the namesake narrator. As night falls on Berlin, young men whistle up to their lovers from the street below Frl. Schroeder's lodging house, wanting to be let in. 'Because of the whistling, I do not care to stay here in the evenings,' he writes.

> It reminds me that I am in a foreign city, alone, far from home. Sometimes I determine not to listen to it, pick up a book, try to read. But soon a call is sure to sound, so piercing, so insistent, so despairingly human, that at last I have to get up and peep through the slats of the Venetian blind to make quite sure that it is not – as I know very well it could not possibly be – for me. (*GB*, 7)

The narrator could simply mean that he is single and thus none of the whistles are for him; at the same time, he seems to foreclose the very idea of emotional connection ('it could not possibly be . . . for me'), as if he were the only homosexual in the world. Indeed, Claude Summers has argued that the theme of *Goodbye to Berlin* is 'the essential loneliness of the human condition', exemplified by the narrator and the other characters he meets.[23] For example, while the young English actress Sally Bowles likes to pretend she is a femme fatale who cynically exploits her male admirers, in reality the film contracts she supposedly trades for her sexual favours never materialize, and Sally is herself beguiled by a conman who pretends to be a film agent and steals her money. She falls in love with a piano player called Klaus, but he abandons her in favour of a job in England, leaving her pregnant. Even her friendship with 'Chris' is a turbulent affair, subject to quarrels and break-ups, and when she leaves Berlin, he never hears from her again, notwithstanding a couple of postcards.

Another example is Peter Wilkinson, an English homosexual who, following a series of nervous breakdowns, comes to Berlin to undergo psychoanalysis. He is another 'truly weak man' who recapitulates traits from Isherwood's earlier characters: like Philip Lindsay, he has a manipulative, mollycoddling mother who contrives to remove him from public school and has him educated by private tutors. Peter's backstory often reads like a parody of the psychosomatic theories of John Layard and Homer Lane. For instance, as a result of repressing an impulse to kill his father with a bread knife, he suffers an uncontrollable facial twitch, and finally has to throw himself 'face downwards on the wet lawn' for fifteen minutes (*GB*, 84). After failing to have sex with a female prostitute, Peter develops a rash on his thigh and an eye infection. It is at this point that he submits to psychoanalysis and ends up in Berlin, where he meets the working-class adolescent Otto Nowak. On learning that Peter has been paying an analyst to talk to him, Otto is incredulous and attempts to cure him with his animal vitality. He counteracts Peter's neurotic misery by putting him into contact with his body through sex, wrestling and sunbathing.

The narrator meets them on Rügen and wryly observes their stormy relationship. 'It is Peter's will against Otto's body,' he writes. 'Otto is his whole body; Peter is only his head. Otto moves fluidly, effortlessly; his gestures have the savage, unconscious grace of a cruel, elegant animal. Peter drives himself about, lashing his stiff, ungraceful body with the whip of his merciless will' (*GB*, 81). This suggests another of Isherwood's early influences: D. H. Lawrence. In fact, the narrator discusses *Lady Chatterley's Lover* (1928) with his female English students, and Peter can be read as representative of the mental-mechanical worldview of Clifford and Connie Chatterley while the proletarian Otto is a German Mellors. But Otto's cure is undermined by Peter's jealousy, for Otto is predominantly heterosexual and makes Peter miserable by flirting with girls and dancing every night at the Kurhaus. Eventually, Otto wearies of their constant fighting and inscribes his farewell note on a blank page torn from Peter's copy of *Beyond the Pleasure Principle* by Freud. Perhaps Otto is meant to embody the pleasure principle while Peter is the doleful custodian of the reality principle. At any rate, Peter resolves to return to London and another round of psychoanalysis, and does not even pretend that he will keep in touch with the narrator.

Bernhard Landauer is another lonely, over-cerebral neurotic like Peter Wilkinson, who manages his uncle's department store in Berlin. The narrator has a letter of introduction to the Landauer family and is moved to get in touch after hearing an antisemitic diatribe from Frl. Mayr on the 'thieving Jews' who own all the department stores and who are 'sucking' the 'life-blood' from the indigenous Aryans (*GB*, 139). Over dinner, the narrator is asked by Herr Landauer whether justice was served in the case of Oscar Wilde and is aware of Bernhard 'discreetly smiling' in the background. Bernhard seems to be attracted to the narrator and invites him to his well-appointed flat, which is filled with exquisite *objets d'art* from his extensive travels. Isherwood gives an odd, Orientalized portrait of Bernhard that emphasizes his passivity, false humility and inanition. Bernhard is wearing a kimono and his profile is described as 'over-civilized'. He eats nothing but tomatoes and rusks and drinks milk; his face is 'masked with exhaustion' and betrays a 'mortal weariness', and the narrator wonders whether he is 'suffering from a fatal disease' (*GB*, 154–5). The implication seems to be that Bernhard's interest in culture, art and religion – he has a sandstone Buddha head from Khmer in his bedroom – has resulted in an atrophy of the body and its appetites, which again is reminiscent of Lawrence.

The last time the narrator visits Bernhard, he finds him looking ill, as if having aged ten years since their previous meeting: 'His face was pale and drawn; the weariness did not lift from it even when he smiled' (*GB*, 176). Bernhard confides that he sometimes feels he doesn't exist; he finds the Nazi menace 'unreal' and does not bother to report the antisemitic death threats he receives to the police. After Bernhard mentions in passing that China is his spiritual homeland, the narrator urges him to go there (his uncle has already left the country and his niece Natalia is living in France). But when Bernhard proposes that they go together and leave Berlin that night, the narrator infers it as a joke, and it is only much later, when he learns that Bernhard has been murdered by the Nazis, that he realizes his offer was sincere. At an earlier garden party at the Landauers' villa, the narrator gazes at the Jewish guests and prophetically reflects that 'all these people are ultimately doomed. This evening is the dress-rehearsal of a disaster. It is like the last night of an epoch' (*GB*, 174).

While Isherwood had his own emotional reasons for being a pacifist that were bound up with Heinz and his father, he sought more rational, universal reasons from Gerald Heard, who had been a prominent member of the Peace Pledge Union (a pacifist organization founded by Dick Sheppard) prior to emigrating to America with the writer Aldous Huxley in 1937. Heard was a multifaceted intellectual who wrote forbidding books with portentous titles – *The Ascent of Humanity* (1929), *The Source of Civilization* (1935), *Pain, Sex and Time* (1939) – that attempted to synthesize science, religion, anthropology, psychology and the paranormal. He was best known to the public as the BBC's Science Commentator. After settling in California, Heard and Huxley had been initiated by Swami Prabhavananda, the head of the Vedanta

Society of Southern California. Given Isherwood's mounting dislike of New York, he was easily persuaded to come to California to consolidate his pacifism.

Isherwood had known Heard since the early 1930s, and had become friends with his partner Chris Wood, whose family business in jam had made him independently wealthy. In those days, Heard had been a sartorial fetishist – his first book was *Narcissus: An Anatomy of Clothes* (1924) – who delighted in stylishly eccentric outfits, whereas the Heard who confronted him in Los Angeles was an ascetic, who had grown a 'Christlike' beard and wore shabby clothes with holes in the knees and patches at the elbows.[24] Heard's interest in Asian religions had gone hand in hand with his commitment to pacifism, and he had alienated some members of the Peace Pledge Union by introducing group meditation sessions. The idea was that one could not hope to promote peace in the world if one hadn't achieved peace within oneself. Heard was now celibate and lived in an annexe of Chris Wood's house overlooking Laurel Canyon, with a bedroom and bathroom. He also meditated for six hours a day and had given up alcohol, meat and fish, subsisting off rotten fruit, dried sandwiches and bits of cake left over from picnics with friends.

While Isherwood was unnerved by this change in Heard, and regarded Eastern spirituality in terms of levitation and fakirs, there was no gainsaying Heard's intelligence. In fact, it helped that Heard expounded his beliefs using the Sanskrit vocabulary of Vedanta, whereas Christian terms (grace, prayer, faith) were polluted by association with the others (bishops, schoolmasters and so on). Heard explained that the universe was an emanation of the Hindu godhead *brahman*, and that the world we see around us, of apparent difference and duality (self and other, mind and body, human and divine), was an illusion (*maya*). The purpose of meditation was to detach oneself from the illusory ego and to realize that the true self (*atman*) is in fact the same as *brahman* – or, put differently, that *atman* is *brahman* in human form. In order to realize this divine self, Heard had systematically set about eradicating the buttresses of the ego: addictions and aversions, material possessions and what he called 'pretensions' – for example, if one took pride in one's asceticism and began to feel spiritually superior to other people (this was always a danger with Heard), the ego would inevitably inflate.

Although far from convinced by Heard's exposition of Vedanta, Isherwood felt adrift in his own life and decided to give meditation a go. Predictably, his mind was assailed by distractions – the ego, sex, noises outside the window – but even though he only practised it intermittently and for short periods of time he acknowledged that meditation had a beneficial effect. Heard introduced him to Swami Prabhavananda, who struck him as sympathetic and 'boyish' despite being in his forties, and whose smile was 'so touching, so open, so brilliant with joy' that it made him 'want to cry' (*D1*, 43). Prabhavananda respected Isherwood's aversion to the word 'God' – referring instead to 'the Self' and 'Nature' – and gave him some basic instruction in meditation. Isherwood sheepishly asked whether the spiritual life was compatible with 'having a sexual relationship with a young man'. Had the Swami answered, as he half expected, that homosexuality was a sin, he would have walked away, but instead Prabhavananda replied: 'You must try to see him as the young Lord Krishna' (*MG*, 25). In other words, Prabhavananda was urging Isherwood to see *brahman* in his lover Harvey Young. Unlike Christianity, a dualistic religion which valorizes the soul over the sinful body, Advaita (literally, non-dual) Vedanta is monistic,[25] and therefore *brahman* is immanent in the body (rather than transcending it, like the Christian God). But while sex (whether heterosexual or homosexual) was not a sin in the Christian sense, if one aspired to enlightenment like Heard (which meant liberation from *samsara*, the relentless cycle of rebirth), chastity was a necessity, for sex was a form of attachment that anchored one to the world of *maya* (ego, duality, difference).[26]

In July Berthold Viertel (the director of *Little Friend*) invited Isherwood to collaborate on a film titled *The Mad Dog of War*, which was to be about a young German who joins the Nazi Party after the First World War but becomes disillusioned with their ideology.

Isherwood enjoyed the Viertel household on Mabery Road, and after batting around ideas for *Mad Dog* in the morning, he and Viertel would swim in the sea before lunch, feeling mildly guilty for enjoying the amenities of Santa Monica while their friends in Europe were bracing themselves for war. When the war came in September 1939, Isherwood recorded: 'No fear, no despair, no sensation at all. Just hollowness' (*D*1, 46). In order to obtain work in America, he had procured a quota visa in June; he'd also applied to become a U.S. citizen, and as such was exempt from British

Isherwood and Swami Prabhavananda at the Hollywood Vedanta Center on Ivar Avenue, early 1940s.

conscription. His plan was to join the American Red Cross at some point and come to Britain in a non-combatant capacity; in the meantime, he would keep working on the film with Viertel.

It didn't take long for Isherwood and Auden's absence to be attacked by the British press. The following poem was printed in the *New Statesman* under the pseudonym 'Viper', but was probably written by Anthony Powell, a right-wing writer who was indignant at Isherwood's celebrity:

> The literary erstwhile Left-wellwisher would
> Seek vainly now for Auden or for Isherwood:
> The dog beneath the skin has had the brains
> To save it, Norris-like, by changing trains. (*D*1, 83)

A journalist in *Reynold's News* disparaged the 'émigré writers Huxley, Heard and Isherwood, who have gone to California to "contemplate their navels"'.[27] In the February 1940 issue of *Horizon*, a new periodical edited by Stephen Spender and Cyril Connolly, the latter noted in an editorial that Auden and Isherwood had applied to become American citizens: 'They are far-sighted and ambitious young men, with a strong sense of self-preservation, and an eye on the main chance, who have abandoned what they consider the sinking ship of European democracy, and by implication the aesthetic doctrine of social realism that has been prevailing there.'[28] A few months later in *The Spectator*, the writer and politician Harold Nicolson accused Huxley, Heard, Isherwood and Auden of selfishly pursuing 'the Wisdom of the East' while 'Western civilization is bursting into flames and thunder.'[29]

These attacks only exacerbated Isherwood's sense of guilt and ramped up his soul-searching. 'Am I a coward, a deserter?' he wrote in his diary. 'Am I afraid of being bombed? Of course. Everybody is. But within reason . . . No, it isn't that . . . If I fear anything, I fear the atmosphere of the war, the power which it gives to all the things I hate – the newspapers, the politicians, the puritans, the scoutmasters, the middle-aged merciless spinsters' (*D*1, 83–4). In his politely angry letter to Spender, who as co-editor

Swami Prabhavananda, Aldous Huxley and Isherwood in the Green House living room at Ivar Avenue, 1948.

of *Horizon* implicitly endorsed Connolly's remarks in the anonymous 'Comment' section, he affirmed: 'Wystan and I probably *will* come over, in an ambulance unit. But this will be an act of pure self-crucifixion. I can't imagine that either of us would be very useful.' He disingenuously added that his decision to become a U.S. citizen was because 'I believe that the future of English culture is in America, and that the building of this future will be assisted by the largest possible cultural emigration.'[30] There followed an epistolary silence of nine months.

Isherwood's newfound pacifism and his interest in Vedanta had also caused a rift in his friendship with Upward, who wrote Isherwood an indignant letter when he learned about this development from Olive Mangeot: 'Pacifism is almost the most pernicious theory you could have chosen. If you had become a Catholic or had decided to believe that the earth is flat I should have been less alarmed.'[31] In his reply, Isherwood explained that he'd become increasingly uncomfortable with his false public persona of committed left-wing intellectual dutifully espousing the party line. This was epitomized by the reception of *Journey to a War*, which was derided by the Left 'because it was messy, personal, sentimental and confused, like myself'. He added:

'That is the way I will always be: personal. So I don't belong to any movement; and I cannot really take sides in any struggle.'[32]

Meanwhile, he had been working on a film adaptation of James Hilton's novel *Rage in Heaven* (1932), and MGM offered him a year-long contract with a salary of $600 a week (about $13,000 today).[33] If anything, the worsening war in Europe and the attacks in the press led Isherwood to commit himself more fully to the spiritual path, and he regularly went to the temple at the Hollywood Vedanta Center on Ivar Avenue to meditate and to hear Prabhavananda lecture. He also saw a lot of Heard during this period, and occasionally attended Alan Hunter's Congregational church, where laypeople such as Heard and Huxley gave spiritual talks. In July 1940 he received the news that Uncle Henry had died, leaving him the Marple estate. He reflected in his diary that it had come 'too late' to make a difference:

> not merely because of the war, but because the absurd boyhood dream of riches is over forever. It is too late to invite my friends to a banquet, to burn the Flemish tapestry and the Elizabethan beds, to turn the house into a brothel. I no longer want to be revenged on the past. (*D1*, 103)

Isherwood graciously decided to turn over the estate and Uncle Henry's private property to his brother Richard, who loved Marple Hall and wanted to live there, and who was currently working on the farm at Wyberslegh Hall to avoid conscription.

That November he formally became Prabhavananda's disciple in an initiation ceremony at Ivar Avenue. Isherwood was given a Sanskrit mantra (a holy name which he was forbidden to disclose) and a rosary to count off the repetitions of his mantra, a process known as making *japam*. During the ceremony, Isherwood made offerings to Ramakrishna, the figurehead of the Vedanta Society. Ramakrishna was a Hindu saint from a poor Vaishnava family. In 1856, at the age of twenty, he was appointed priest of the Kali Temple at Dakshineswar. He studied many different religions during his lifetime, Hindu philosophies as well as Islam and Christianity, and he affirmed that all religions led to God.³⁴ After his death in 1886, his most dynamic disciple Swami Vivekananda set about establishing the Ramakrishna Order to disseminate his guru's teachings. In 1893 Vivekananda travelled to Chicago to represent Hinduism at the World Parliament of Religions. His speech was enthusiastically received and he remained in America for the next few years proselytizing Vedanta, eventually establishing the Vedanta Society of America. After his death in 1902, Swami Brahmananda became head of the Ramakrishna Order: Prabhavananda was Brahmananda's disciple, just as Isherwood was now Prabhavananda's disciple.

In the temple, there was a photograph of Ramakrishna and an icon of Christ. One of the tenets of Vedanta is that 'all religions are essentially in agreement.'³⁵ At first blush Christianity, with its emphasis on the duality of God and humans, would appear to be incompatible with the monism of Advaita Vedanta, which holds that *atman* and *brahman* are one. Some Christian saints, however, practised mental prayer or contemplation, which is analogous to meditation, and experienced a mystical union with God, in which state their ego (with its stubborn insistence on separate selfhood) was dissolved. For example, the German theologian Meister Eckhart wrote:

> For it is of the very essence of the soul that she is powerless to plumb the depths of her creator. And here one cannot speak of the soul any more, for she has lost her nature yonder in the oneness of divine essence. There she is no more called soul, but is called immeasurable being.

And: 'The knower and the known are one. Simple people imagine that they should see God, as if He stood there and they here. This is not so. God and I, we are one in knowledge.'³⁶

The unitive state described by the Christian mystics is strikingly similar to what the Hindus call *samadhi*, which is the ultimate goal of meditation. For instance, in the Mandukya Upanishad, *samadhi* is described as: 'pure unitary consciousness wherein awareness of the world and of multiplicity is completely obliterated. It is ineffable peace. It is the Supreme Good. It is One without a second. It is the Self.'[37] The term 'self-realization' denotes the ecstatic recognition that there is no difference between one's self and 'the Self' (that is, *brahman*). Furthermore, Ramakrishna regarded key figures from other religions, such as Buddha and Christ, as avatars of *brahman* – hence the icon of Christ in the Vedanta shrine alongside the Hindu deities and the Buddha.

At the start of 1941 Prabhavananda and Heard had a falling out. Heard dissociated himself from the Vedanta Society on the grounds that Prabhavananda's lifestyle was insufficiently monastic, complaining that the Swami ate meat, smoked cigarettes, drove a car and was pampered by the Vedanta nuns. There was always a degree of ostentation in Heard's asceticism, and Isherwood noted in his diary that despite Gerald's threadbare clothes he lived in comfort with Chris Wood and enjoyed books, food and transport from his friends. In addition, though Isherwood was unaware of this, Heard had inherited a substantial sum of money from his friend and former employer Sir Horace Plunkett,[38] and was planning to start his own spiritual community, which may have played a part in his quarrel with Prabhavananda. In response, Prabhavananda wrote an indignant article for *Vedanta and the West* (the magazine that Heard had helped to edit) in which he argued that renunciation is a state of mind and that a beggar may be fiercely attached to his trifling possessions while a king may be non-attached to his fortune. Isherwood deplored the rift, and diplomatically sat on the fence. 'On the one side,' he noted in his diary, 'apparent disorder, religious bohemianism, jokes, childish quarrels, dressing up in saris, curry, cigarettes, oriental laissez-faire; on the other, primness, plainness, neatness, austerity, discreet malice, carrots, patched blue jeans, wit and western severity . . . Gerald offered me discipline, method, intellectual conviction. But the Swami offered me love' (*D1*, 151).

The following month Isherwood and Harvey split up. Part of the problem was sexual – Harvey was also attracted to women and for a long time their relationship had been more or less platonic.[39] There was also the difference in their ages, with Harvey protesting that Isherwood didn't take his painting seriously and was always patronizing him. Isherwood moved to Green Valley Road, not far from where Gerard Heard was now living on Arlene Terrace. Under Heard's influence, he became more ascetic and quit smoking. Furthermore, for the past year he'd been on a strict diet of fresh fruit and vegetables under the auspices of the Vedanta devotee Dr Kolisch, and had given up fish, meat and alcohol. This was meant to alleviate indigestion, depression and 'nervous headaches', but despite his dietary restrictions Isherwood complained that his 'stomach [wa]s cramped in a tight knot of hate and fear' (*D*1, 92–3). It's odd that Isherwood, who as a former disciple of John Layard and Homer Lane subscribed to psychosomatic explanations, never seems to have blamed the war for his condition.

When Isherwood's contract with MGM expired in May 1941, he made no effort to renew it. Around this time, Denny Fouts came to stay with him in his annexe on Green Valley Road. Fouts would inspire the character of Paul in *Down There on a Visit*, where he is described as 'the most expensive male prostitute in Europe' (*DTV*, 206). Isherwood had briefly met Fouts in London and reconnected with him the previous autumn in Los Angeles. As a hard-drinking former heroin addict, Fouts was burnt out and was curious about Isherwood's conversion to Vedanta. But when Isherwood introduced him to Prabhavananda, the Swami recommended hard work rather than religion. Fouts was deeply hurt by Prabhavananda's rejection, so Isherwood introduced him to Heard, who immediately recruited him for the monastic community Heard was calling Focus (it would eventually be known as Trabuco College). Heard arranged for Fouts to work on a farm in Pennsylvania so he could use the experience to grow food on the Focus land (Heard was still looking for a promising plot). When Fouts had finished his stint on the farm he returned to LA and began living with Isherwood, who was more than willing to cohabit with this alluringly 'wolflike' man. Nonetheless, they attempted to lead a monastic life, meditating for three hours a day and reading religious literature in between their sits. But they 'didn't give up thinking about sex, talking about sex' or bragging about their 'glamorous love lives' (*D*1, 156).

Heard had cultivated contacts with the Quaker community. In July Isherwood and Fouts participated in a religious retreat in the small town of La Verne, east of Los Angeles. The La Verne Seminar had been organized by Isherwood's cousin Felix Greene, a journalist who was working for the American Friends Service Committee (AFSC) in Philadelphia. The purpose of the month-long seminar was to debate the respective merits of social work and contemplation. Isherwood had himself undertaken some social work with the AFSC, delivering clothes to Oklahoma climate migrants in California, but Heard's group maintained that social work only benefitted the doer, in terms of karma, and that contemplation was paramount. For Heard, the ultimate goal of life was to achieve enlightenment by turning away from the world in meditation and directly experiencing the undifferentiated *brahman*. Failure to achieve this end would result in rebirth, and Heard was disgusted with life. In black moods, he regarded the world as a quagmire of evil and corruption. On one occasion he horrified Isherwood by describing the penis as 'like a bit of loose gut hanging down from the abdomen' (*MG*, 76). One of his favourite reproaches was to describe someone as having 'a tremendous *grip* on life', implying that they were attached to the world and its tawdry trinkets, instead of practising non-attachment like himself.

By the end of the seminar, Isherwood had concluded that the contemplative life was not for him and that social work was more congenial. Later that August, Fouts was sent to the San Dimas camp in the San Gabriel Valley, where conscientious objectors could undertake forestry work, but Isherwood was too old for the peacetime draft. Instead, he used his Quaker contacts to obtain voluntary work at an AFSC hostel for refugees in Haverford, Pennsylvania. Here Isherwood's fluent German proved invaluable and his principal job was giving English lessons. He got on well with the German refugees and made detailed character sketches of them in his diary, obviously anticipating a later fictional treatment.

He faithfully attended the Quaker Meetings on a Sunday, but the puritan side of his nature was always at war with the pleasure principle. On Christmas Day 1941 he took a train to New York and

Aum shrine in Trabuco grounds, photograph taken by the author in August 2023.

got horribly drunk with his former lover Harvey, indicating that during this time he was far from teetotal. Indeed, his outward Quaker rectitude was further eroded the following year, when Pete Martinez, a Mexican ballet dancer whom Isherwood had met in New York, began working at the hostel while waiting to be conscripted. Martinez was put in Isherwood's room and they soon became lovers. When Martinez left towards the end of April, Isherwood was relieved that he could return to a semblance of Quaker propriety, but the hostel closed a few months later, partly for financial reasons.

During Isherwood's time at Haverford, Heard had realized his plans for a spiritual community on a large plot of land in the hills behind Laguna Beach in Orange County, California. He had enlisted the help of Isherwood's cousin Felix Greene, in whose hands Heard's original idea of a small retreat for half a dozen people had metamorphosed into an elegant monastery, called Trabuco College, that could house fifty. Heard conceived of Trabuco as a nondenominational 'club for mystics' and as 'a clearinghouse for individual religious experience and ideas'

(*D*1, 235). Although there was supposed to be no hierarchy of masters and disciples, it was inevitable that Heard would be the leader. In the Trabuco prospectus, co-written with Huxley, it is stated: 'The founders do not regard themselves as possessed of any special message or esoteric "revelation." Trabuco begins its work in a spirit of humble and open-minded enquiry. There are no "prophets" among us.'[40] In other words, Heard was not presenting himself as an enlightened sage, dispensing wisdom that had been gleaned first-hand from mystical union.

The daily schedule at Trabuco consisted of three hour-long meditation sessions, three meals and a spell of maintenance or gardening work in the grounds during the afternoon. Heard hoped that Trabuco would become a wholly self-sufficient anarchist community, which grew its own food and was not dependent on the outside world. The original plan had been that the residents would examine the 'enormous mass of existing literature, from many countries and ages, on techniques of prayer, ways of self-integration and methods of psycho-physical

The monastery exterior at Trabuco.

development', test these techniques and, if they proved efficacious, incorporate them into the Trabuco regime.[41] But while there was a library of religious literature at Trabuco, none of the residents reported conducting this kind of purposive research. According to one resident: 'Gerald talked during and after every meal, sometimes for hours . . . The topics were life and spiritual life. He spoke as a guru.'[42]

When Isherwood visited Trabuco in July, it wasn't quite finished and he stayed with Chris Wood, who had moved to Laguna Beach to be near Heard and had bought a magnificent house built into a cliff overlooking the Pacific Ocean. With the American entry into the war, following the bombing of Pearl Harbor in December 1941, the age limit for conscription had been raised to 44, which meant that Isherwood had to apply for a 4-E classification as a conscientious objector. While waiting to be drafted into a Civilian Public Service camp in Santa Barbara, Isherwood divided his time between Los Angeles and Laguna Beach, with occasional trips to Trabuco. He had expected to be called up at any moment, but when he still hadn't heard anything in September 1942, he applied to be reclassified as a theology student, which would mean he would be able to help Prabhavananda with his translation of the *Bhagavad Gita*.

After a weekend seminar at Trabuco on prayer, Isherwood wrote in his diary:

> If I really desire God more than anything else, then I must desire my periods of prayer more than anything else. (I most certainly don't.) And if I believe that God is Reality, then I must regard my prayer periods as real, or approximately real, and the gaps between them as less real. (*D*1, 247)

For Isherwood at this time, though, it was the body and the material world which struck him as real, and while his meditation practice had produced beneficial effects, in terms of concentration and well-being, it had not stripped the world of its illusory multiplicity and revealed it as the ineffable *brahman*. On the one hand, even zealous meditators like Heard had not attained the ecstasy of *samadhi*; on the other, Isherwood felt that he might make more spiritual progress if he was shielded from the temptations of the world.

With this in mind, he resolved to move to Ivar Avenue in the New Year and undertake monastic training. Another motivation for this step was to shore up his status as a theology student, but shortly afterwards the conscription ceiling was lowered to 37, and he was now 38. Although Isherwood admitted that, had it not been for the unpalatable prospect of working at the Civilian Public Service camp, he 'would probably never have actually signed on with the Swami', he chose to regard it as the machinations of karma and went ahead with his training (*D*1, 261). He was due to move into 'Brahmananda Cottage', a new house acquired by the Vedanta Center on Ivar Avenue and repurposed as a monastery, on 6 February 1943. In his diary, Isherwood contemplated his new monastic life with all the serenity of someone facing a long prison sentence. During the last days of his freedom, he resolved to write a new novel, made a valedictory walk around Santa Monica, fantasized about a last hurrah with a young serviceman and visited a garish nightclub on the Sunset Strip.

The birthday of Swami Brahmananda, Prabhavananda's guru, was 6 February. In 1923, a year after Brahmananda's death, Prabhavananda was sent by the Ramakrishna Order to be an assistant swami at the San Francisco Vedanta Center. While lecturing in Los Angeles a few years later, he met Carrie Mead Wyckoff, whose interest in Vedanta had been piqued by Swami Vivekananda back in 1900. She was now a widow and offered Prabhavananda the use of her house on Ivar Avenue in order to form a new Hollywood Vedanta Center. Over the next decade the congregation slowly expanded, and in 1938 enough money had been raised to build an onion-domed temple in Wyckoff's garden, which contained a small lecture hall, living quarters for the swami and a shrine. Brahmananda Cottage was the latest addition to the Vedanta Center, and was used as a monastery for the male initiates while Wyckoff's house was used by the Vedanta nuns. Isherwood lived with two teenaged boys, a man named George Fitts and the Swami's nephew Asit Ghosh, who, after studying cinematography at the University of Southern California, had been unable to return to India because of the war.

Isherwood's schedule at Ivar Avenue consisted of meditation periods in the morning and evening. He was also expected to make *japam*, repeating his mantra in front of the shrine at least 2,500 times a day. In addition, Isherwood participated in more elaborate ritual worship in the temple, which included food and floral offerings to Ramakrishna and the deities in the shrine, a purification ceremony and various prayers, which lasted an hour and a half. He performed domestic duties, such as washing up, and helped Prabhavananda to edit the magazine *Vedanta and the West*, which featured articles by Heard, Huxley and the playwright John van Druten (a fellow expatriate and friend). But his chief literary chore was to help Prabhavananda translate the *Bhagavad Gita*.

The *Gita* (*c.* second century BCE) is one of the principal texts of Hinduism, and relates the discourse between the Pandava warrior Arjuna and Sri Krishna (an avatar of Vishnu who has taken human form as Arjuna's charioteer). Arjuna is about to go to war with the Kaurava army, but is dismayed when he perceives his teachers and relatives in their ranks. Believing it is morally wrong to slay his kinsmen, Arjuna lays down his arms. Krishna explains that while the body can be killed, the *atman* is immortal: 'Not wounded by weapons,/ Not burned by fire,/ Not dried by the wind,/ Not wetted by water:/ Such is the Atman.'[43] Just as the *atman* of Arjuna will be untouched by the death of his body, so will the *atman* of his kinsmen; therefore, Krishna tells him, he should not mourn their death. Furthermore, as a warrior it is Arjuna's *dharma* (spiritual duty or divine law) to fight. Krishna dilates on the three spiritual paths that lead to enlightenment: *jnana yoga* (the path of wisdom), *bhakti yoga* (the path of devotion) and *karma yoga* (the path of action). For Arjuna, *karma yoga* means fighting against the Kauravas, but he can avoid the spiritual demerit that redounds on killing kinsmen by practising non-attachment. 'To unite the heart with Brahman and then to act,' Krishna proclaims, 'that is the secret of non-attached work. In the calm of self-surrender, the seers renounce the fruits of their actions, and so reach enlightenment.'[44] It is through desire and attachment to mundane things – power, possessions, sex and so on – which are transient and ultimately 'unreal', that people fail to apprehend 'the Real' (*brahman*).

In his daily life at Ivar Avenue, though, Isherwood often fell short of this philosophical certitude. 'Real are my sex fantasies and memories,' he wrote in his diary. 'Real are the devices I think up for not being woken by Asit's alarm clock. Utterly, utterly unreal are Ramakrishna, religion, the war with all its casualties and suffering, and the problems of other people' (*D*1, 306). When not engaged in spiritual work, Isherwood was free to come and go as he pleased, and during this period he made frequent trips to visit Aldous and Maria Huxley at their new home in the Mojave Desert, Llano del Rio, as well as Chris Wood and Heard at Laguna Beach. He also saw a lot of Berthold Viertel and the writer Dodie Smith. In addition, he'd made a start on his next novel, *Prater Violet*, after having written nothing but a couple of indifferent short stories during the last four years.

On 6 August Isherwood celebrated six months of 'technical celibacy', by which he meant that while he had refrained from physical congress, he had thought about sex an awful lot. He decided to take a break from Ivar Avenue and rented a room in Santa Monica. One day on the beach, he stripped off his trunks while in the sea and slung them round his neck for safekeeping; a passing stranger, inferring this as an invitation, took off his trunks and entered the sea. After a spell of mutual masturbation, Isherwood pulled away, not wanting to ejaculate, as if this would mitigate his breach of celibacy. Back in his room, he finished off the job himself, but felt 'no pleasure'. He was wretched after the lapse, and returned to Ivar Avenue two days early. The most galling aspect was that his vanity was hurt because he could no longer be proud of his celibacy. The following month he had another casual encounter on the beach with a frisky young man, who ambitiously essayed an underwater blowjob, claiming he could breathe by sucking air through Isherwood's cock, and grew indignant when he almost drowned.[45] A few days later, Isherwood slept with Pete Martinez, his former lover from Haverford, who was on leave from the army.

He finished his translation of the *Bhagavad Gita* in February 1944. At first, he'd attempted a stolidly faithful prose version, but after some negative feedback from Huxley, he decided to break up the prose with a more spacious, alliterative verse, and set to work with renewed enthusiasm. With the *Gita* put to bed, Isherwood resumed work on *Prater Violet*, which had stalled after a couple of pages. One of his anxieties during this period was that Prabhavananda would give him a Sanskrit name, as he had done with most of the other devotees (Amiya, Sudhira, Yogini and so on), and he would brood on this possibility while supposedly meditating. 'I feel sure I'm not going to be a member of the Ramakrishna Order, or any kind of monk,' he wrote in his diary. 'I've got to be C. Isherwood, and that's that' (*D*1, 351). In other words, he was jealously guarding his identity as a writer while simultaneously striving, through meditation, to transcend his ego and identifywith *brahman*.

Much like the previous year, he vacillated between periods of spiritual tranquillity and turmoil. 'I am very happy to be without sex,' he noted in his diary in March, 'oh, much more than happy, utterly thankful' (*D*1, 337). A few days later, though, he reported: 'The thought of sex hovers in the background, like potential panic amongst the audience in a theater where there is no fire escape' (*D*1, 339). These sex thoughts had been exacerbated by Bill Harris, a dreamy blond with Olympian legs whom he'd met through Denny Fouts. He became obsessed with Harris, whom he referred to as 'X.' in his diary, as if his name were so magically potent that, like the Tetragrammaton, it could not be spoken out loud. Unfortunately, Isherwood found that having sex with Harris only aggravated his obsession.

Despite 'the X. situation', Isherwood was able to focus on literary work. He collaborated with Huxley on a film treatment about a spiritual healer, titled *Jacob's Hands*, which didn't get produced but was published in 1998 after the actress Sharon Stone read about the project in Isherwood's diaries and approached Huxley's widow Laura, who found the manuscript in a box of souvenirs. Isherwood corrected the proofs of the *Gita* translation in June; edited and wrote an introduction to an anthology of articles that had appeared in the magazine *Vedanta and the West*; in between times he had been working on *Prater Violet*, which he finished in October. In his diary entry for New Year's Eve 1944, he struck a note of spiritual serenity: 'Suddenly, I feel quite calm. Sure, the situation is impossible. Sure, I ought to stop seeing X., or leave Ivar Avenue, or both. I ought either to get a movie job or start a new story. But the whole problem . . . has to be accepted for what it is, and simply offered up,' that is, to God. 'Make japam, watch and wait' (*D*1, 379).

5
Samsara, 1945–53

In February 1945 there was an article in *Time* magazine devoted to Isherwood and Prabhavananda and their translation of the *Gita*. Isherwood felt acutely uncomfortable that he was being portrayed as a Vedanta monk when in reality he was merely living at Ivar Avenue while leading a decidedly secular life in Santa Monica. After Bill Harris moved to New York, Isherwood began an affair with a messenger boy from Warner Bros who gave him gonorrhoea. It was shameful, he reflected, having to return to the monastery after visiting a 'v.d. clinic'. In addition, he was now working on a screenplay of Wilkie Collins's novel *The Woman in White* (1860). In order to justify his generous salary, he was required to keep regular office hours at Warner Bros. In retrospect, he could only recall participating in a single *puja* that year, and he meditated, if at all, for a few minutes in the mornings before work.[1] He keenly felt the hypocrisy of his position, but whenever he broached the subject of leaving the monastery, Prabhavananda would persuade him to stay, obviously hoping that his errant disciple would eventually embrace the monastic life.

The messenger boy was a mere *amuse-bouche* until a more substantial lover came along in the form of Bill Caskey. The 24-year-old Caskey was a mercurial character who'd been discharged from the U.S. Navy for homosexual activities. On the one hand, he was 'outspoken, crude, vulgar' and occasionally 'violent'; on the other, he could evince a 'southern upper-class charm to go with his Kentucky accent' and looked dashing in a suit (*LY*, 42). A good example of Caskey's social dexterity comes from a dinner party hosted by Charlie Chaplin; one of the guests naively expressed her pleasure in being seated next to Caskey by saying: 'I always like sitting next to a pansy.' This was greeted by a 'deathly silence', but Caskey saved the situation by wittily remarking: 'Your slang is out of date, Natasha – we don't say "pansy" nowadays. We say "cocksucker"' (*LY*, 235). Musing on his affair with Bill Harris, Isherwood reflected that Harris was 'too feminine' for his taste, which required a certain 'coarseness', such as chest hair or a 'roll of fat' (*LY*, 20). In contrast, Caskey had a masculine pelt over his chest and back, bad teeth and a 'biggish cock' (*LY*, 42).

Isherwood finally left Ivar Avenue on 23 August 1945. In *My Guru and His Disciple*, he maintains that his relationship with Caskey provided the impetus, but elsewhere he stated that he was angry with a friend for 'bitchily pretending to think that Caskey was the reason why Christopher had left the Vedanta Center' (*LY*, 45–6). Aside from Caskey, it cannot be a coincidence that the Japanese had surrendered nine days earlier, on 14 August, effectively ending the Second World War. As a prominent pacifist who'd been excoriated by British critics for emigrating to America, he must have wanted to account for his actions during the war by pointing to his work at the refugee hostel in Haverford and his monastic training at Ivar Avenue. This was perhaps why he'd submitted an essay about the La Verne Seminar to *Penguin New Writing* in 1942, when its editor John Lehmann was obviously hoping for more fiction in the manner of *Goodbye to Berlin*. This was why he'd begun a novella about his time with the Jewish refugees at the Quaker hostel. Furthermore, *Prater Violet* features a Jewish refugee whose Cassandra-like prophecies about the Nazi apocalypse fall on deaf ears; after it was published in November 1945, presented it as the first part of a projected trilogy of novellas about the plight of Jewish refugees.[2]

On the back cover of the American edition of *Prater Violet*, the author's note states that Isherwood had gone 'into virtual literary retirement' during the war and that he'd 'devoted himself to mystical studies while living monastically in Hollywood'.[3] Even though Isherwood wrote most of the novel in 1944, there is some truth in this statement, for there's no obvious literary reason why he couldn't have written *Prater Violet* in 1939 (apart from the ending, which will be discussed below). As early as 1935, he had been planning to use his experience with Viertel in a sprawling, never-completed novel titled *Paul Is Alone*. If one of the reasons Isherwood had moved to the United States was to continue to write, free from the tedious war work that would be meted out to friends in England, his guilty conscience may have been responsible for his writer's block.

Prater Violet begins not long after the end of *Goodbye to Berlin*, in the autumn of 1933, with the namesake narrator living in Kensington with his mother and brother and receiving a mysterious summons from Imperial Bulldog Pictures to work on a musical film titled *Prater Violet*. In the phone call with the secretary from Imperial Bulldog, it emerges that the narrator has lived in Berlin and speaks fluent German, which will help him work with the film's Austrian director Friedrich Bergmann. There follows a charming scene over the breakfast table, in which the narrator feigns indifference at the prospect of working on a film; his brother Richard marvels at his sangfroid; while his mother sees through the pretence but indulges him. After the slighting reference to Kathleen as his 'female relative' in *Lions and Shadows*, and the conspicuous absence of the narrator's family in *Mr Norris Changes Trains* and *Goodbye to Berlin*, this affectionate portrayal of domestic life indicates that the war, or just the passage of time, has palliated the old grudges.

When the narrator meets Bergmann for lunch, he likens him to a 'tragic Punch' and perceives in his harried features the 'face of Central Europe' (*pv*, 15). While 'Isherwood' pontificates to his mother about the possibility of Hitler invading Austria, his glib analysis suggests that for him nothing is at stake: 'I used a lot of my favourite words: Gauleiter, solidarity, démarche, dialectic, Gleichschaltung, infiltration, Anschluss' (*pv*, 6). But for Bergmann, as a Jew with socialist sympathies who has left his wife and children in Austria, this possibility is all too real, and he persistently prophesizes war:

Bill Harris (a.k.a. 'X.', lying on the sand) Bill Caskey (seated) and Isherwood, 1946, by Alec Beesley, in an imitation of John Everett Millais's *The Boyhood of Raleigh* (1870).

> The attack on Vienna, Prague, London and Paris . . . the conquest of Europe in a week . . . the massacre of the Jews, the execution of intellectuals, the herding of non-Nordic women into enormous state brothels; the burning of paintings and books . . . the establishment of Brown Art, Brown Literature . . . Brown Science and the Hitler Religion, with its Vatican at Munich and its Lourdes at Berchtesgaden. (*PV*, 38)

Despite the vividness and conviction of Bergmann's evocations, the idea of another European war is as unimaginable to the narrator as his own death.

The plot of the novel, such as it is, follows Isherwood's experience of working on *Little Friend*, and some of the best lines and incidental details are derived directly from Viertel. For instance, after meeting the narrator, Bergmann says: 'You know, already, I feel absolutely no shame before you. We are like two married men who meet in a whorehouse' (*PV*, 21). Bergmann is impressed with Blake's suicide attempt in *The Memorial*, and comments: 'This I find clearly genial' (*PV*, 24), using the German meaning of the word *genial*, which denotes 'gifted with genius'. Bergmann repeatedly claims he is a 'Jewish Socrates' who will die for telling the truth and accuses the narrator of being a 'typical mother's son' (*PV*, 26).[4] On the other hand, the film they are making bears no resemblance to *Little Friend*, and concerns a prince who falls in love with a violet seller in the Prater, a public park in Vienna. When Bergmann extrapolates a political message from the film, his words, ostensibly referring to the prince, are aimed by the author at his younger self:

> He is unable to cut himself free, sternly, from the bourgeois dream of the Mother . . . He wants to crawl back into the economic safety of the womb. He hates the paternal, revolutionary tradition, which reminds him of his duty as its son. His pretended love for the masses was only a flirtation. (*PV*, 47)

Earlier in the novel, the narrator is mortified that he cannot write dialogue for the working-class characters of the film, because for all his 'parlour socialism' he is a 'snob' who is only conversant with the language of 'public-school boys and neurotic bohemians' (*PV*, 32).

The second half of the novel revolves around shooting the film. The narrator notes that his memories of this period are bereft of any sequence or chronology, and gives an impressionistic, present-tense account of the shoot that evokes the particularity of the sets and lighting as well as the personalities of the technicians, who regard the film-making process as a deadly serious game. The narrator's job is the same as Isherwood's had been – dialogue director – and this involves mediating between Bergmann and the studio executives. All goes well until the eruption of the Austrian Civil War in February, which throws Bergmann (who is worried about his wife and children) into despair, and the idea of working on a sentimental musical during this time strikes him as obscene. When a journalist tells Bergmann that it is unreasonable to expect the British people to care about the civil war in Austria, Bergmann explodes: 'I expect this whole damned island to care! I will tell you something: if they do not care, they will be made to care. The whole lot of you. You will be bombed and slaughtered and conquered.' Bergmann looks to the narrator to respond, but he can't. 'I knew what I was supposed to feel,' he reflects:

> what it was fashionable for my generation to feel. We cared about everything: fascism in Germany and Italy, the seizure of Manchuria, Indian nationalism, the Irish question, the workers, the Negroes, the Jews. We had spread our feelings over the whole world; and I knew that mine were spread very thin. I cared – oh, yes, I certainly cared – about the Austrian socialists. But did I care as much as I said I did, tried to imagine I did? No, not nearly as much. (*PV*, 99)

The civil war lasts less than a week, and while the socialists are defeated Bergmann learns that his family is safe. After a fortnight of reckless directorial indifference, his passion for the project revives and he finishes the shoot in a whirl of hectic brilliance.

The final scene of *Prater Violet* has led some critics to describe it as a religious novel. After the party to celebrate the end of the shoot, the narrator and Bergmann walk through the deserted pre-dawn streets of Chelsea. Bergmann is silent and the narrator shies away from asking the crucial questions: 'What makes you go on living? Why don't you kill yourself? Why is all this bearable?' (*PV*, 117). If he were asked these questions, he muses, he would answer love; he then gives a very clear-eyed vision of his present affair with 'J.', and how it will inevitably end, leading him to act out the same drama with 'K. and L. and M.' The corollary being that love is not enough. But then how to assuage the fear of war and death, and 'the arch-fear: the fear of being afraid' (*PV*, 119)? Turning onto Sloane Street, he experiences an epiphany: 'And, at this moment,' he writes,

> like the high far glimpse of a goat track through the mountains between clouds, I see something else: the way that leads to safety. To where there is no fear, no loneliness, no need of J., K., L., or M.

> For a second, I glimpse it. For an instant, it is even quite clear. Then the clouds shut down, and a breath off the glacier, icy with the inhuman coldness of the peaks, touches my cheek. 'No,' I think, 'I could never do it. Rather the fear I know, the loneliness I know . . . For to take that other way would mean that I should lose myself. I should no longer be a person. I should no longer be Christopher Isherwood. No, no. That's more terrible than the bombs. More terrible than having no lover. That I can never face.' (*PV*, 119)

The 'way' he glimpses above is the Vedantic way, which maintains that the ego is an illusion that blinds us to the undifferentiated reality of *brahman*. If we accept that humans, and everything else in the universe, are an emanation of *brahman*, there can be no death or fear or loneliness. *Brahman* can never die, and we can never be isolated or cut off from *brahman* because *everything is brahman*. But for all his hours of meditation before the shrine at Ivar Avenue, Isherwood had been unable to transcend his ego, and *brahman* remained a tantalizing abstraction. Moreover, the idea of taking a Sanskrit name at Ivar Avenue had been anathema because he was unwilling to renounce his literary identity: 'To me, "Christopher Isherwood" was much more than just my name; it was the code word for my identity as a writer, the formula for the essence of my artistic power. So, to force me to take another name would [have been] an act of hostile magic' (*MG*, 158).

Ultimately, it was his desire to be Christopher Isherwood, rather than an anonymous Vedanta monk, that led him to leave Ivar Avenue. What he took with him was, as he put it in *My Guru*, a 'faith in Swami's faith' (*MG*, 337). One of the chief attractions of Vedanta and Ivar Avenue was Prabhavananda, a father figure like E. M. Forster, whose love and approbation he cherished. At the end of the novel, Bergmann occupies the guru position of Prabhavananda: 'Beneath outer consciousness, two other beings, anonymous, impersonal, without labels, had met and recognised each other, and had clasped hands. He was my father. I was his son. And I loved him very much' (*PV*, 121). In reality, Isherwood's affection for Viertel at this time was vitiated by the latter's homophobia, and he'd left the shoot before its end to be with Heinz in Amsterdam. It was only later, in 1935, when a common friend had informed Viertel of Isherwood's sexual orientation, and Viertel had shown that he was willing to respect it, that they became good friends.

In September 1945 Denny Fouts moved to New York, after a brief stint studying medicine at UCLA, and sublet his apartment on Entrada Drive to Isherwood and Caskey. Looking back, Isherwood could not remember writing in this apartment, for he was too busy partying and nursing hangovers to get any work done. While Caskey was seventeen years younger than Isherwood, he was very much his own man, who, unlike Isherwood's previous partners, did not require his guidance and protection. If anything, Caskey was the more dominant partner. Where Isherwood had previously been a feisty top, he now submitted to being a bottom. 'Caskey would strip and put on a pair of cowboy boots,' Isherwood recalled. '"You want to get the shit fucked out of you?" he would ask' (*LY*, 56). But because Caskey was even smaller than Isherwood this macho persona lacked conviction. They frequently quarrelled when drunk, and would occasionally come to blows. As a former navy man, Caskey was stronger than Isherwood and rarely retaliated; indeed, according to Isherwood, he derived a 'deep sensual satisfaction' from his bruises and black eyes (*LY*, 52).

In the New Year Isherwood consulted a doctor about a painful constriction in his penis. The doctor diagnosed an obstruction at the junction of the bladder and urethra. Isherwood was feeling guilty for his failure to become a monk and regarded this problem as a condign punishment. After the anaesthetic was administered, the doctor asked for Isherwood's consent to perform a vasectomy to prevent infection; such was Isherwood's confusion that he thought the doctor had asked whether he was planning on becoming a 'parrot' rather than a 'parent'; when his dopey patient replied that this was impossible, the doctor went ahead with the procedure. Dr Kolisch, the Vedanta physician, told him that the vasectomy had been completely unjustified, and predicted that it would eventually leave him impotent. In the short term, though, it had an invigorating effect on Isherwood's libido, and he began to frequent a secluded area called 'the pits' on Santa Monica State Beach, where middle-aged homosexuals sunbathed in the nude and had sex. He and Caskey enjoyed a polyamorous relationship, which worked out well for both partners, as long as Caskey showed no signs of emotional attachment. Caskey's preference was for heterosexual men, who, paradoxically, didn't object to being blown or buggered by Caskey. He exasperated Isherwood by grading these men '1A', while Isherwood, as a homosexual, was a '1B' (*LY*, 54).

Isherwood became an American citizen on 8 November 1946. In the process, he took the opportunity of dropping his cumbersome middle names, as if purging himself of his English heritage and becoming one with his author persona. In the New Year he decided to return to England for a visit. He superstitiously chose 19 January 1947 to leave (this was the date he'd set out for China with Auden in 1938 and the United States in 1939), but he couldn't have chosen a less propitious time for his trip. England was inundated with snow in one of the worst winters in many years, with temperatures plummeting to -21°C (-6°F). In the aftermath of the war, the country was still rationing food and fuel. To aggravate matters, there were now power cuts because the snow drifts prevented coal being delivered to power stations. All of which came as a nasty shock to Isherwood, who had grown acclimatized to the balmy California winters.

Nevertheless, he received a warm welcome from his friends in London. 'You enter the room and there they all are,' he wrote. 'There is a moment of dreamlike unreality. Then constraint and uneasy politeness. Then the tremendous, poignant shock of recognition.'[5] Whatever apprehensions he might have had prior to the trip concerning his reception, he affirmed that none of his friends betrayed the least resentment about his absence during the war. He felt obliged, however, to exaggerate his faint American accent (he'd made an effort to flatten his vowels on arriving in America, with the result that he was often assumed to be Australian), in order to demonstrate that despite his British past he was now a U.S. citizen. There were numerous parties held in his honour, as well as lunches, dinners and drinks with old friends and former boyfriends, including Forster, Jean Ross, Olive Mangeot, Gerald Hamilton, Stephen Spender and Edward Upward. He eagerly hoovered up compliments about his perennial youthfulness while noting how antique his friends appeared in comparison.

Perhaps the greatest transformation time had wrought was on his brother:

> Richard's face looked mad and somehow psychologically *skinned*, all its protective coverings stripped away down to the raw, the quick of defenseless misery . . . His clothes were aggressively dirty, stained with food and smeared with coal dust. He took so many laxatives for fear of constipation that he would sometimes shit in his bed. (*LY*, 87)

A few years after Uncle Henry's death, Kathleen and Richard had moved back to Wyberslegh, which had been their home in the early years of Kathleen's marriage. It seems probable that Richard, given his obsessive behaviour and learning difficulties, was on the autistic spectrum, and after dropping out of several schools he'd been unable to go to university or find a job. To avoid conscription during the war, Richard had volunteered for work on the farm at Wyberslegh, and had let his personal hygiene slide. He made no effort to wipe his nose and exaggerated his cough to court Kathleen's attention. 'But he was neither childish nor mad,' Isherwood concluded, 'he was a sensitive, intelligent soul in torment' (*LY*, 87).

Due to the snow drifts, Isherwood was stuck indoors for most of his month-long stay at Wyberslegh. Kathleen had had a gas fire specially installed in Isherwood's bedroom, but as a result of gas rationing it generated little heat, and even with his overcoat on it was too cold to sit still and read. He spent many hours with Kathleen in the kitchen (the warmest room in the house) regaling her with stories of his life in Los Angeles. Fortunately for Kathleen, she was a patient listener and by skirting contentious issues such as politics they got on well.

Back in America, he finally began the novel about the Haverford refugees, titled *The School of Tragedy*, but quickly ground to a halt. Partly in response to old-fashioned critics like Forster, who frowned on Isherwood's self-referentiality, he'd resolved to jettison his namesake narrator, but this entailed creating a convincing authorial stand-in who could carry the cargo of his experience while also being a straight American. This was the same issue that had stymied his aborted novel *Paul Is Alone*, and he set it aside in favour of a travel book on South America, *The Condor and the Cows* (1949). Caskey would provide the photos (having recently completed a photography course in Santa Monica), and Isherwood hoped that the book would kickstart his career.

They embarked on their South American trip in the autumn of 1947, taking a ship from New York to Venezuela. The only record of this period is *The Condor and the Cows*, which is narrated by a sanitized 'Christopher Isherwood', a sexless camera like Herr Issyvoo whose lens is trained outward rather than inward. Bill Caskey is presented as 'the photographer', whose relationship with Isherwood is purely platonic. In each city, Isherwood met with the U.S. Ambassador and the director of either the American or the English Cultural Institute, who would in turn introduce him to the region's writers and artists. He produced dutiful reports of each country's economic and political situation, and dutifully described the cultural landmarks – the Inca citadel at Machu Picchu, the San Francisco church and monastery at Quito – but his heart wasn't in it. Every so often, there is a flash of Isherwood's descriptive brio. For example, in Barrancabermeja in Colombia he spots two alligators: 'They squatted half awash on the edge of the water, their mouths slightly open with an air of contented depravity.'[6] But these flashes only serve to underline the pedestrian nature of the rest of the narrative. 'I just cannot do straight journalism,' he wrote to John Lehmann, lamenting his struggles with *The Condor and the Cows*, 'and the truth is that South America *bored* me, and I am ashamed that it bored me, and I hate it for making me feel ashamed.'[7]

From South America, they sailed to Europe, where they reconnected with Denny Fouts, who was now addicted to opium

W. H. Auden, Stephen Spender and Isherwood on Fire Island in 1947, by Bill Caskey. This is a recreation of the 'famous' photograph of them taken by Spender on Rügen Island in 1931.

and leading a spectral existence in Paris. On meeting Fouts at the Ritz, Isherwood likened him to 'Dorian Gray emerging from the tomb – death-pale and very slim in his dark elegant suit . . . like the Necropolitan ambassador' (D1, 402). At Fouts's urging, Isherwood smoked some opium, but disliked the taste and affirmed that it had no discernible effect. He felt that Fouts was resentful of his relationship with Caskey, and tried to stir up trouble by asking Caskey to score some opium from a dealer, which Isherwood vetoed, fearing that Caskey might be arrested. Regrettably, this quarrel was the last time Isherwood saw Fouts, who died of a heart attack eight months later. In Les Deux Magots (a literary brasserie formerly patronized by Hemingway and Joyce), Isherwood made the acquaintance of Gore Vidal. Vidal had sent him the manuscript of his latest novel, *The City and the Pillar* (1948), for a puff, which Isherwood had provided, even though he didn't care for the book. He described Vidal as 'a big husky boy with fair wavy hair', who 'reminds me of a teddy bear' (*D*1, 401). After noticing Vidal's 'very sexy legs' one morning at breakfast, he became quite smitten, and inferred from Vidal's flirtatious manner that he felt the same way, but Vidal (who was 22 at the time) later recorded that Isherwood was too old for him.[8]

At the end of September 1948, Isherwood and Caskey moved into a house on East Rustic Road in Santa Monica, but their relationship was unravelling. Caskey's bullish self-assertion, while initially attractive, was exhausting over the long haul. They were also at different stages of life: where Caskey wanted to stay up drinking all night and playing records, Isherwood wanted to go to bed at a reasonable hour and write in the mornings. And when Isherwood complained, Caskey doubled down on his selfish behaviour. The following year Isherwood noted in his diary that he was 'verging on some kind of a nervous breakdown' (*D*1, 411). As with Heinz and Harvey, no matter how miserable and irredeemable his relationship with Caskey became, he was unable to end it. For some reason, he imagined that if they split up he would either have to return to Ivar Avenue or would be doomed to live alone, when in fact Isherwood estimated that he'd slept with over four hundred men and showed no signs of slowing down.

Their dysfunctional relationship dragged on for another two years, during which time Isherwood made several false starts with *The School of Tragedy*. Things finally came to a head with Caskey during a party in May 1951: Isherwood was too drunk to remember what happened, but he moved out the next day and took up residence at a writers' retreat, the Huntington Hartford Foundation. The previous year he'd been befriended by a literary wunderkind named Speed Lamkin, who'd published his first novel at the age of 22 and who was on the board of the Foundation. Lamkin was also at the retreat, and Isherwood gave him his latest draft of *The School of Tragedy*. Lamkin's verdict – 'the refugees are a bore'[9] – was liberating, for he abruptly perceived that he'd been writing two novels: one about the lapsed Quaker Stephen Monk, his failed marriage and wanting to assuage his conscience by working at the hostel, and the other about the Jewish refugees, who would now have to be expunged.

Contrary to expectations, Isherwood adjusted well to living alone. He had a small stable of sex partners, and with Caskey gone, he was finally able to make some progress with his novel. He spent most of May 1952 at Trabuco, which was now owned by the Vedanta Society of Southern California. Heard had hoped that Trabuco would become a model of anarchist self-sufficiency, producing its own food, but by 1947 there were too few residents to cultivate the land and he was forced to close it. Moreover, as a former resident put it, Trabuco did not generate the 'spiritual outcomes [Heard] had hoped for', and he regarded this as a 'failure'.[10] Heard had long ago reconciled his differences with Prabhavananda, and he donated Trabuco to the Vedanta Society. Isherwood found the healthy regimen at Trabuco, with its early nights and meditation spells, conducive to work and here he completed another collaboration with Prabhavananda: a new translation of the *Yoga Sutras* of Patanjali, titled *How to Know God* (1953).

The *Yoga Sutras* (*c.* second–third century CE) is a seminal Hindu text. As the Sanskrit *sutras* (literally 'threads') are short, Patanjali's text is outweighed by Prabhavananda's commentary on them. The yoga system is divided into eight limbs. Nowadays, yoga has come to be associated with the *asanas* or postures, which constitute the third limb of yoga, but when Patanjali refers to *asanas* he means seated postures such as the lotus pose (*padmasana*) rather than headstand or downward-facing dog.[11] A good seat (*asana*) is essential for meditation (*dhyana*, the seventh limb). In the second *sutra* of the first *pada* (foot or section), Patanjali states: 'Yoga is the control of thought-waves in the mind.'[12] Only when the yogi has mastered meditation can the final limb, *samadhi*, be attained. In contrast to Advaita (non-dual) Vedanta, the yoga tradition is starkly dualistic, divided into *prakriti* (the world, the body *as well as* the mind) and *purusha* (the divine self). For Patanjali, there are several stages of *samadhi*, in which the yogi systematically dissociates his self from the relative, impermanent realm of *prakriti* and identifies with the eternal, immutable consciousness of *purusha*. 'Then man abides in

Gerald Heard, Isherwood and Swami Prabhavananda at Trabuco, *c*. 1950.

his own nature,' affirms Patanjali in the third sutra. 'Such a man', adds Prabhavananda in his commentary, 'is known as a free, illumined soul.'[13]

The following year Isherwood began a relationship with Don Bachardy, an eighteen-year-old freshman at UCLA. He had spotted Don and his older brother Ted on the beach at Santa Monica. At first it was Ted, and in particular Ted's legs, that attracted Isherwood, and they slept with each other a couple of times.[14] After a Valentine's Day party in 1953, however, it was Don who went home with Isherwood. So began a relationship that would last the rest of Isherwood's life. Shortly afterwards, Ted (who suffered from manic-depressive schizophrenia) began to exhibit symptoms of a psychotic break, and his parents ended up calling the police, who 'dragged [him] away, screaming and fighting, in handcuffs'. To distract Don from his brother's suffering, Isherwood took him to Palm Springs. 'I feel a special kind of love for Don,' he wrote in his dairy. 'There's a brilliant wide-openness about his mouse face, with its brown eyes and tooth gap and bristling crew cut, which affects everybody who sees him. If one could still be like that at forty, one would be a saint' (*D*1, 454).

Isherwood finally completed his novel, now titled *The World in the Evening*, in August 1953. When the novel appeared the following year, the book sold well in spite of hostile reviews. One of the problems with the novel is the character of the narrator Stephen Monk. Noting his reflection at a Hollywood party in 1941, he describes himself as 'a tall blond youngish-oldish man with a weakly good-looking, anxious face' (*WE*, 11). This oxymoronic evocation illustrates the fatal indeterminacy of Monk's character: he is both gay and straight, young and old, American and English. In Part One especially, the narrator's prose awkwardly attempts to reflect Monk's Anglo-American heritage. 'The party, that evening, was at the Novotnys'. They lived high up on the slopes of the Hollywood hills, in a ranch-style home complete with Early American maple, nautical brasswork and muslin curtains; just too cute for words' (*WE*, 11). The final clause, with its emphatic American idiom, feels bolted on and out of kilter with the rest.

After catching his second wife Jane having sex with one of the guests, Monk drives home drunk, takes a razor to Jane's wardrobe, scrawls some expletives on the mirror with her lipstick and throws up.

Trabuco lecture hall, with a portrait of Ramakrishna on the wall. Taken by the author in August 2023, the hall is essentially unchanged since Isherwood's day.

This trite melodrama seems unwarranted when we learn, much later, that Monk goaded Jane into cheating on him to bring their joyless marriage to an end. But in Part One, Monk is obsessed with Jane, which Isherwood telegraphs with some artless interior monologues: 'Jane, Jane, Jane, Jane. Suddenly it had started up inside me again, like a toothache. Jane, where are you now? Aren't you thinking about me? Don't you want me back?' (*WE*, 33). Monk seeks refuge with his Quaker aunt Sarah Pennington in Dolgelly, Pennsylvania. Sarah is delighted to see him and her naive estimation of his goodness causes Monk to feel even more guilty for the aimless, hedonistic life he has been leading in Hollywood. After Sarah takes him to the Quaker Meeting, Monk decides to leave, vaguely thinking he will enlist in the Canadian Army (this being some months prior to the attack on Pearl Harbor). But one of Monk's most consistent character traits is that he is a coward who forces those around him to act and make the decisions, and, en route to the railway station, he contrives to get himself run over by a truck.

After the disappointment of Part One (subtitled 'An End'), Isherwood goes some way to redeeming the novel in Part Two ('Letters and Life'), only to unravel his good work in Part Three ('A Beginning'). As a result of breaking his thigh in the 'accident', Monk must undergo ten weeks of bedrest in a body cast. He is nursed by a German refugee named Gerda Mannheim, whose husband enlisted in the French army and was captured by the Nazis. The example of Gerda's unflinching fortitude makes Monk feel ashamed of his egocentric marital misery: 'All through this last year, the War had existed merely as a loud, ugly appropriate background music for my expensive private hell. Why shouldn't London blaze, why shouldn't Jews be tortured, why shouldn't all Europe be enslaved, as long as the great tyrant Me was suffering?' (*WE*, 28).

The enforced bedrest gives Monk the opportunity to peruse the letters of his first wife Elizabeth Rydal, who died in 1935, which precipitates a Proustian remembrance of things past. Isherwood drew on the letters of Katherine Mansfield for the character of Elizabeth,[15] who is on the fringes of the Bloomsbury group and socializes with Virginia Woolf and Mary Scriven from *The Memorial*.

Don Bachardy and Isherwood, July 1953.

Isherwood deftly limns the early years of their marriage but runs into problems when attempting to depict Monk's infidelities. For no discernible reason, the hitherto uxorious Monk becomes a remorseless lothario. When a young man named Michael Drummond confesses his love, Monk affects to be disgusted – 'I'm not that way, and I won't ever be' – but decides to have sex with him anyway. 'I rationalized my shameless physical itch, transforming it into a big noble generous gesture, a gift of princely charity from myself, who had everything, to Michael, who had nothing at all' (*WE*, 226). Next, he cheats on Elizabeth with Jane, a vacuous American who is holidaying in St Luc. Elizabeth has a heart condition, much exacerbated by a miscarriage. Sensing that the end is nigh, she begs Monk not to go to Marseille (where he has a rendezvous with Jane), but he manoeuvres Elizabeth into begging him to make the trip, and she dies a few days later.

Initially, Isherwood had conceived of Monk as bisexual because he wanted him to be different from himself, but didn't feel confident in creating a heterosexual narrator. But Isherwood's prejudice against married bisexuals clearly influenced his portrayal of Monk. In a letter to John Lehmann, he explained that Monk's infidelity was designed 'to vent my spleen against wicked bisexuals who break the hearts of innocent queens and then go waltzing back to Wifey'.[16] Indeed, in writing about the married bisexual Stephen Monk, Isherwood may have been channelling his feelings about the married bisexual Stephen Spender.[17] When Spender had left his partner Tony Hyndman in 1936 to marry a woman he'd known for less than a month, Isherwood had felt betrayed. The marriage broke down a few years later due to Spender's open affairs with men, but he married again in 1941. Isherwood later described Spender as 'deeply false' and 'utterly untrustworthy' in connection with his bisexuality.[18] And so it made sense that the bisexual Monk 'must cheat in every possible way on everybody'.[19]

While Monk is recuperating in bed, Isherwood imposes on him some religious insights born of his Vedanta studies, but which are inconsistent with Monk's Quaker background.

> Lying there, in the almost mindless calm of first waking, I felt as if I could remember everything I'd ever done or said or thought since I was a baby. Only this wasn't exactly remembering. Memory pieces things together gradually, making a chain; this was total, instantaneous awareness. The thousands of bits of my life seemed to be scattered around me, like the furniture of the room, all simultaneously present. I wasn't young, I wasn't old; I wasn't any particular age or any particular I. Everything particular was on the outside; and what was aware of this was a simple consciousness that had no name, no face, no identity of any kind. (*WE*, 109–10)

In the yoga tradition of Patanjali, this consciousness that transcends the everyday sense of self and that exists as a witness to the individual's actions and thoughts throughout her life is known as *purusha*. The *purusha* takes a karmic audit of the individual, and will be reborn for those who die with outstanding karmic debt, which is carried over into the next incarnation;

liberation is only possible, then, for individuals whose selfless deeds have amortized their bad karma. Isherwood alludes to *purusha* in the title of the novel, which derives from the opening lines of John Donne's poem 'The Progress of the Soul':

> I sing the progress of a deathless soul,
> Whom Fate, which God made, but doth not control,
> Placed in most shapes; all times before the law
> Yoked us, and when, and since, in this I sing.
> And the great world to his aged evening;
> From infant morn, through manly noon I draw.[20]

As Elizabeth approaches death, she too is visited with Vedantic wisdom. 'I could never make very much out of church-religion,' she writes to Mary Scriven.

> But still I do believe in Him – or in my version of Him, which I prefer to call 'It'. At least, I'm sure now . . . that there's a source of life within me – and that It can't be destroyed. I shall not live on, but It will . . . I, like everything else, am much more essentially in It than in I. (*WE*, 260)

In other words, her true self (the *atman*) is not the ego or the mortal body but *brahman*. That both Monk and Elizabeth become independently aware of these Vedantic insights is implausible.

The cast on Monk's leg is likened by his doctor Charles Kennedy to a chrysalis, out of which Monk will emerge like a 'gorgeous butterfly'. This is an obvious metaphor for Monk's metamorphosis from self-indulgent rich boy to the selfless pacifist who enlists in an ambulance unit bound for North Africa in Part Three. The protagonist's pacifist conversion had originally been conceived as one of the novel's main subjects, whereas now it takes place off-stage. Kennedy's boyfriend, Bob Wood, visits Monk in Part Two, and discovers that they have a lot in common. They both believe in God but dislike the sanctimonious Quakers who worship Him, and who wilfully ignore the uncomfortable fact that Wood and

Kennedy are more than wholesome housemates. Despite renouncing his Quaker faith, Wood is drawn towards pacifism as the war approaches. When he asks if Monk is a pacifist, Monk replies: 'Kind of. I haven't ever thought about it properly' (*WE*, 119). But by Part Three, Monk has committed himself to the pacifist cause and joined an ambulance unit, presumably having been inspired by the goodness and charity of Gerda and Aunt Sarah, while Wood has been called up by the navy and has decided to fight: 'I thought to myself: I can't be a C.O. because, if they declared war on the queers – tried to round us up and liquidate us, or something – I'd fight. I'd fight till I dropped . . . So how can I say I'm a pacifist?' (*WE*, 310).

Brian Finney has argued that Isherwood's homosexual characters are included for 'propaganda purposes' but are superfluous to the narrative.[21] Certainly, the relationship between Kennedy and Wood (while far from perfect) can be favourably contrasted with Monk's marriages. Furthermore, Wood embodies Isherwood's antipathy towards the 'heterosexual majority'.[22] He tells Monk that he could have exempted himself from the navy if he'd told them he was queer, but he refused. 'Because what they're claiming is that us queers are unfit for their beautiful pure Army and Navy – when they ought to be glad to have us' (*WE*, 311). Likewise, Kennedy articulates some of Isherwood's reservations about the Quakers. For instance, he complains that the Friends 'lack style' and have 'no notion of elegance'. Through Kennedy, Isherwood ventriloquizes a definition of high camp a decade prior to Susan Sontag's essay 'Notes on "Camp"': 'High Camp always has an underlying seriousness. You can't camp about something you don't take seriously. You're not making fun of it; you're making fun out of it. You're expressing what's basically serious to you in terms of fun and artifice and elegance' (*WE*, 125). Until the unlikely advent of 'Quaker camp', homosexuals such as Kennedy and Wood (and, one suspects, Isherwood) will feel out of sympathy with the Friends.

There's an oddly manic quality to Part Three, which may express Isherwood's relief in finally finishing the novel, and he engineers a spurious happy ending for his characters. Monk enjoys a drunken evening with Wood and Kennedy, with lots of jaunty badinage, even though Wood is about to depart for the front. Gerda receives a letter from her husband Peter, who has miraculously escaped the Nazis, while Monk and Jane (who is about to embark on another marriage) reconcile over cocktails in New York. The novel ends on a bathetic note: '"Do you know something, Jane," I said, as I emptied my glass, "I really do forgive myself, from the bottom of my heart?"' (*WE*, 333). This is a line that Isherwood had uttered to a friend about sin, making them both laugh, but on the page, as he later admitted: 'one doesn't laugh. One is embarrassed' (*LY*, 227).

6
Kitty and Dobbin, 1954–64

In February 1954 Isherwood and Bachardy moved into an apartment on Mesa Road in Santa Monica. It was a mark of Isherwood's fervour for Bachardy that he'd given up the numerous sex partners he'd been seeing. Furthermore, he punched the director Curtis Harrington in the face after one of his friends attempted to seduce Bachardy at a party, which would cost him many legal headaches, much embarrassment and $350 in damages. In the Isherwood mythos, Bachardy was 'Kitty', an affectionate white kitten who could also scratch (when for instance Isherwood and his friends treated him like a child), while Isherwood was 'Dobbin', an old grey workhorse, and together they were 'the Animals', united in their hatred and opposition of 'the others' – that is, the people (mostly heterosexuals) who disapproved of their relationship.[1]

It was perhaps an indication of Isherwood's domestic stability that he turned fifty that August with admirable aplomb. 'Fifty – the unimaginable age', he recorded in his diary. 'And now comes what might be the most interesting part of life – the twenty years till seventy. What shall I do with them?' (*D*1, 465). During a trip to Mexico with Bachardy and some friends in December, he got the inspiration for a new novel about a Kafkaesque journey in which the characters were dead, which would eventually become *Down There on a Visit*. However, the reviews of *The World in the Evening* had been poor and confirmed what he'd feared all along: 'I can't write an "I" who isn't me.' In *World*, he had 'tried to call Stephen "I" and just hope for the best', and this had resulted in a character who was only sporadically convincing.[2] Instead of pushing ahead with a new novel, he signed a contract with MGM in January 1955 to write a biopic of the Buddha, titled *The Wayfarer*. As if to compensate, he resolved to write in his diary twice a week for a year, having all but stopped keeping a diary during the chaotic years with Caskey.

But Isherwood was unable to enjoy his Hollywood lucre without feeling guilty. The death of Maria Huxley from breast cancer in February was an unsettling memento mori: 'I cried all the way to the studio,' he wrote after her funeral, 'and I was really crying for myself' (*D*1, 478). After his friend the photographer George Platt Lynes was diagnosed with lung cancer a few months later, the hypochondriac Isherwood began to worry that a persistent headache indicated a brain tumour. The previous year he'd begun taking vitamin and hormone injections, ostensibly for 'acute nervous tension', but also in a bid to boost his vitality. 'How I wish this Easter could be a complete renewal for me!' he wistfully noted in his diary. But in the absence of a Christlike resurrection, he predicted that 'middle age is going to be just a waning of powers, a narrowing, an increase in squalor – messy – better brought to a quick close' (*D*1, 489).

Although life with Bachardy was a lot quieter than with Caskey, there was an endless succession of parties, lunches, boozy afternoons on the beach. After a heavy night in New York in October, he complained of 'an almost paralytic hangover – the kind which makes you fear you'll lose your nerve in the middle of the street and have to park the car and scream for help' (*D*1, 535). For the most part, Bachardy was a loving partner but prone to fits of spleen when Isherwood's friends didn't treat him as an equal. He'd dropped out of UCLA and had worked for a while as an apprentice for one of Isherwood's Hollywood friends to learn set design, but this had ended in acrimony. In order to cheer him up, Isherwood took him on a European tour after completing his script for *The Wayfarer* in October.

In Rome, Isherwood visited the grave of Denny Fouts and was once again afflicted with intimations of mortality. 'Europe, in its autumn, reminds me of my own,' he wrote in his diary. 'And I seem to myself to look older every day. And I feel no ripening, no resignation. I don't want to get old or die' (*D1*, 550). After touring Venice and Florence, they visited Somerset Maugham and his partner Alan Searle in Cap Ferrat. Maugham had consulted with Isherwood and Prabhavananda while researching his novel *The Razor's Edge* (1944), and *Time* magazine had disseminated the myth that the protagonist, the spiritual seeker Larry Darrell, had been inspired by Isherwood. Maugham was naturally sympathetic to Isherwood's relationship with Bachardy, since Searle was 31 years younger than Maugham, who was now in his eighties.

In London for the New Year, Isherwood was delighted with his friends' decrepitude and noted that 'John [Lehmann] and Stephen [Spender] both look terribly fat in the face – round swollen red bladders' (*D1*, 565). Bachardy had been irascible, so Isherwood decided to visit Wyberslegh alone. As usual on these trips, he was horrified by the appearance of Richard, whom he regarded as a sort of Mr Hyde to his Dr Jekyll: 'Stooped over, with head bowed, he came toward me, looking down and away. Then he threw his head back, and his eyes closed as if he were blind as he turned his face to the sky. His cheeks are rough red and his nose quite purple' (*D1*, 570). Whether consciously or not, Isherwood tended to visit Wyberslegh in winter, when it was at its bleakest – the kitchen coated in grime and coal dust, its closed windows sealing in the damp and the fetor of cooking fat, the surrounding fields mantled in snow. In such circumstances, it was only natural to reflect: 'This is my native country. Thank God for it – and thank God, *on my knees*, that I got out of it!' (*D1*, 573).

Isherwood was anxious about how Bachardy was coping by himself in London, and was reassured to receive a letter from him: 'I miss rides through London on old Dobbin', wrote Bachardy (a.k.a. Kitty),

> and think a lot about him, sleeping in a strange stable, eating cold oats out of an ill-fitting feed bag and having no cat fur to keep him warm . . . tell him an anxious Tabby is at the mercy of the RSPCA and counting the days till his return.[3]

On the last day of his visit, Richard took his brother round Marple Hall, which he'd last seen in 1948 with Bill Caskey. 'Then it was dilapidated. Now it is a ruin – indeed, it has an almost gutted look, as though it had been bombed and burned' (*D*1, 576). One of the chimneys had fallen through the roof, all the windows were smashed, and anything of value had been looted or vandalized. The park was bordered by 'red brick villas' and the council had earmarked some of the land for a new school.

Back in America, Isherwood purchased his first house for $20,000 at 434 Sycamore Road in Santa Monica, which wiped out his savings and rekindled his financial worries. Here he fell into a rewarding domestic life with Bachardy: writing a first draft of a new novel (tentatively titled *The Forgotten*), researching the biography of Ramakrishna he'd agreed to write for Prabhavananda, cooking and tending to the garden. At the beginning of June 1956 Isherwood was diagnosed with hepatitis (which he'd caught from Bachardy) and was hospitalized for over a week. The disease roiled up his fears of old age and infirmity and provided the unsettling insight that 'one might quite well die asking: is *that* all?' (*D*1, 620). After being released from hospital, Isherwood was told that he couldn't drink alcohol for six months, which enhanced his productivity and gave his liver a well-earned rest. Around this time, Bachardy enrolled in the Chouinard Art Institute in Los Angeles. His frequent outbursts in London had partly been due to his not having a career, but now that his artistic talent was being nurtured he was more content.

For much of 1957, Isherwood was afflicted with a series of ailments that were then inflated by his hypochondria. For a start, he was suffering from impotence, which he ascribed to hepatitis. He developed a pain in his thumb that sent shooting pains up his arm and eventually forced him to abandon writing in longhand. In February he had a lump removed from his stomach, which he was certain was cancerous, but which turned out to be benign. He now weighed over 68 kilograms (150 lb), and repeatedly bewailed his burgeoning waistline. He developed chronic indigestion in April, accompanied by a bloated stomach, which he suspected was cancer. Finally, in July, a specialist informed him that his stomach troubles stemmed from his vagus nerve, and prescribed belladonna, but his symptoms persisted for the rest of the year. He was also struggling with his mental health. In March he reported a 'Black depression', largely due to his ongoing impotence with Bachardy, and feared that he might never recover. He grew enraged by the sound of children playing in the neighbourhood (unless, of course, they happened to be cute boys), and fantasized about killing them. But it wasn't just the local kids who were anathema: 'I hate everybody,' he reported in his diary: 'lady drivers, children, cops, Jews, journalists, etc. etc. Never mind about the moral side of this. The point is, if I don't stop I shall make myself seriously ill' (*D*1, 709).

His novel was also causing him problems. He'd completed the first draft of *The Forgotten* towards the end of 1956, but was dissatisfied with it. As with *The World in the Evening*, he was having difficulty deciding who the narrator was, vacillating between the first and the third person, and for a while he considered co-opting William Bradshaw from *Mr Norris Changes Trains*. His original idea was a retelling of the *Inferno*, with a writer named William (the up-to-date Dante), who was being guided through Mexico (a metaphorical hell) by the disreputable Paul (the Virgil figure). He was also eager to recuperate the material about the refugee hostel in Haverford that he'd cut from *The World in the Evening*, and there were a couple of sketches, which had been intended for earlier books, one of Kathleen's cousin Basil Fry (whom he'd visited in Bremen in 1928) and another of Turville-Petre on St Nicholas in 1933, which could be extricated from his diaries. He now perceived that this material could be incorporated into *The Forgotten*: in Mexico, William and Paul would encounter numerous expatriates, representing the damned, and these would include Basil Fry, Turville-Petre and the Jewish refugees.

It wasn't until the start of 1959 that he finally abandoned the *Inferno* allegory and began to construct *Down There on a Visit* out of the wreckage. He decided to use his namesake narrator from *Goodbye to Berlin* and *Prater Violet* to write self-contained character studies of Fry, Turville-Petre and the refugees from the perspective of the present (in which they were all dead), rather than encountering them in a hellish Mexico. In addition to the presence of the namesake narrator, the character of Waldemar would be included in each section to add continuity. With the new structure in place, Isherwood worked rapidly, and had finished the first section ('Mr Lancaster') in less than a month.

In August Isherwood and Bachardy took a trip to Europe. 'Of course, I don't really *want* to go,' the intrepid Isherwood recorded in his diary. 'I wish it were over, but I'll enjoy it, I guess' (*D*1, 822). As usual, they stayed with John Lehmann in London, who was thrilled with 'Mr Lancaster', regarding it as a return to form; Lehmann published it in the *London Magazine*, where it was widely admired. For the first time since he'd emigrated to America, Isherwood visited Wyberslegh during the summer, but this did nothing to palliate the squalor of the place, nor the pathos of its inhabitants. 'Black sooty cobwebs everywhere', Isherwood reported in his diary. 'The walls cracked. The wallpaper hanging in tatters. The carpets stiff with greasy grime.' Richard's appearance was always a shock: he had a 'wild look of dismayed despair', had lost some teeth and was 'dirtier than ever' (*D*1, 823). Kathleen was now ninety years old and had suffered a stroke the year before; while she had made a good recovery, her speech was slightly affected and she now, he noted, smelled of pee. When he said goodbye, he intuited that it was for the last time and ran back into the house for a final embrace.

Back in Los Angeles, Isherwood began his first teaching job at Los Angeles State College. He taught twice a week, focusing on nineteenth- and twentieth-century English texts, including *After Many a Summer* (1939) by Huxley – the novel that his English professor George teaches in *A Single Man*. For all his youthful anti-establishment bluster about Laily and 'the combine', Isherwood had become a don, not to please his mother, but because he needed the money. He had pursued a few film and TV projects during 1959, but these had come to nothing. Moreover, at the end of September, he moved into 145 Adelaide Drive, where he would live for the rest of his life. It was a boutique, split-level house (built in 1926) nestled in the south side of Santa Monica Canyon, which afforded fine views of the sky and the Pacific Ocean, but required extensive renovation.[4]

Although Isherwood harboured doubts about his aptitude for teaching, he eagerly accepted another semester's work for the following year.

He spent the first few days of the new decade getting drunk and vowed to 'give up puritanism for the sixties' (*D1*, 841). Nonetheless, 1960 would be a productive year for Isherwood. He'd begun writing the Ramakrishna biography, which was now being serialized in *Vedanta and the West*. He completed a first draft of the 'Ambrose' section of *Down There on a Visit* in March. Feeling that the novel needed a new section that reflected the mood of the Munich crisis of 1938, he dredged his diaries for material and wrote what would be titled 'Waldemar' in less than five weeks. In comparison, the final section of *Down There* ('Paul') proved troublesome. The character of Paul was inspired by Denny Fouts, and in this section, largely set in 1940, Isherwood wanted to portray his involvement with Gerald Heard and his work at the refugee hostel. In order to boost his productivity, Isherwood was taking Dexamyl, which combined the amphetamine Dexedrine with an anxiolytic called Miltown, which Bachardy had been taking for anxiety and depression. Dexamyl also suppressed appetite and helped Isherwood with his ongoing efforts to lose weight, which had hitherto taken the form of short spells of sobriety, skipping lunch and swimming in the ocean. He finally finished 'Paul' in August, and set about writing a frame narrative that would tie together the disparate sections.

Meanwhile, Kathleen had died on 15 June. 'There is nothing to be said about this at present,' he wrote in his diary. 'I am sad, yes, but I don't really feel M.'s loss. Perhaps I never shall; perhaps I've been through it already' (*D1*, 863). He told himself that he couldn't afford to return to England, but the truth was that he didn't want to go. Kathleen had been the centre of Richard's life, and now that she was dead and Isherwood was living in Los Angeles, he was utterly bereft. Isherwood had asked Amiya (a former Vedanta devotee from Ivar Avenue) to help with the funeral arrangements. While she was out buying flowers, Richard drank the best part of a bottle of whisky and passed out; when salt water was administered, he vomited up a large number of 'pep pills'.[5] Despite a prodigious hangover the next day, Richard got drunk before the funeral and sat through the service in a stupor.[6] On the day Isherwood received Amiya's letter relating these events, he got 'utterly plastered' with the British director Tony Richardson, fell down some steps and slipped a disc.

Bachardy had now finished his studies at the Chouinard and had been having some success selling drawings of Isherwood's celebrity friends. In January 1961 a wealthy patron offered to pay for Bachardy to study in Europe. Stephen Spender pulled some strings with the painter William Coldstream, and Bachardy was admitted to the Slade School of Fine Art for six months (where Coldstream was a professor). After Don's departure, Isherwood attempted to fill the void by working out at a gym, making *japam* and revising *Down There on a Visit*. He also saw a couple of his occasional lovers, but these compared unfavourably with Bachardy, with whom he now had an open relationship. The following month, he announced that he was now 'absolutely impotent' and wondered whether this was due to 'old age, or just that all the gism has gone into novel writing' (*D2*, 51).

In his letters to Bachardy, Isherwood assumed his 'animals' persona: 'Dobbin seems to catch hints in Kitty's letters of concern about possible *riders* Dobbin may be finding? Kitty is not to worry. If anyone tries to get a firm seat on the saddle, Dobbin rears and they go flying off again.'[7] He was haunted by the idea that 'Kitty' might find a younger, more virile stablemate in London, leaving 'old Dobbin' high and dry. After delivering a short series of lectures at UCLA, he flew to London in April. Bachardy was living in Hampstead, in the house of Richard Burton, who was currently playing King Arthur in the Broadway musical *Camelot*.[8] Here Isherwood's anxiety over Bachardy was replaced by a crotchety loathing of London. There was the endless socializing to contend with – the long lunches at 'those eternal Italian restaurants' with their fattening food and 'sleepy red wine', which ruined his fitness regimen (*D2*, 67). The weather was predictably terrible. And while it was wonderful to be reunited with Bachardy, the old issues quickly reasserted themselves, chief among them the fact that Don could never make his own friends because they were instantly beglamoured by Isherwood.

Despite these local difficulties, he made good progress with his revisions of *Down There* and submitted it to his publishers in June. After the chastening experiment of 'writ[ing] an "I" who is not me' in *The World in the Evening*, *Down There* represents a welcome return to autofiction. Indeed, it's an even more sophisticated melange of fact and fiction than *Prater Violet*, in that Isherwood includes the pseudonymous Hugh Weston (Auden), Stephen Savage (Spender) and Allen Chalmers (Upward) from his memoir *Lions and Shadows* (Chalmers also appears in *All the Conspirators*); in addition, there are cryptic references to real authors, such as 'E. M.' (Forster) and 'John' (Lehmann), and the namesake narrator grew up in 'Chapel Bridge' and lived in 'the Hall' like Eric Vernon in *The Memorial*. In an interview, Isherwood confided that 'my work is all part of an autobiography,' and *Down There* both extends the narrative beyond *Prater Violet* and fills in some of the gaps left by previous books.[9] The 'Mr Lancaster' section of *Down There* is set in 1928, and fictionalizes Isherwood's stay in Bremen with his cousin Basil Fry, which had originally been intended for inclusion in *Lions and Shadows*. 'Ambrose' picks up the narrative where *Goodbye to Berlin* left off, in May 1933, and finishes just before the events of *Prater Violet*. 'Waldemar' is set in the autumn of 1938, and depicts Isherwood's despair during the Sudeten crisis; while 'Paul' starts in 1940 and takes us up to 1953.

Although Isherwood had abandoned the idea of rewriting the *Inferno*, the *Down There* of the title alludes to J.-K. Huysmans' novel *Là-bas* (1891), and each section of the novel depicts the private hell of the titular character.[10] Mr Lancaster is a distant relative who manages a shipping company in north Germany. At their first meeting, the 23-year-old 'Isherwood' regards him with contempt: 'As far as I was concerned, everyone over forty belonged, with a mere handful of honorable exceptions, to an alien tribe, hostile by definition but in practice ridiculous rather than formidable' (*DTV*, 4). However, when Lancaster exhorts him to let go of 'your Lady Mother's apron strings' and visit him in Germany, the narrator has no choice but to accept. On closer acquaintance, Lancaster proves to be a Mortmerish representative of 'the others', who glorifies the First World War and endorses stuffy Victorian virtues. On learning that the narrator has just published a novel, he offers to underline all the split infinitives. 'I could have been a writer,' he declares. 'I had that power which only the greatest writers have – the power of looking down on all human experience with absolute objectivity.' His unwavering 'conviction' unnerves the narrator, who is put in mind of 'the way the dead talk about themselves in Dante' (*DTV*, 33).

When Lancaster warns his nephew away from Berlin, which he paints as a latter-day Sodom, the narrator immediately resolves to go there. In *Christopher and His Kind*, Isherwood affirms that he omitted the Bremen trip from *Lions and Shadows* because he was 'unwilling to discuss its sexual significance', and adds that when he used this material in 'Mr Lancaster' it was written with 'too much fiction and too little frankness' (*CK*, 3). What he means is that in *Down There* his namesake narrator is portrayed as a slightly unconvincing heterosexual rather than a fully fledged queer. For instance, en route to Germany, the captain of the company boat gives the narrator a pornographic novel, full of hackneyed descriptions of 'ripe breasts', which 'excited [him] hotly' (*DTV*, 263). There's some homoerotic horseplay in the swimming pool with Waldemar (a young man who works in Lancaster's office), but it's implied that the narrator has sex with a woman (while Waldemar and his friend Oskar watch). And the narrator's sketchy heterosexuality causes narrative problems later in the novel.

On returning to London, his mother tells him that Lancaster's wife left him many years ago because he was impotent. A few months later, the narrator learns that Lancaster has shot himself, which contradicts his initial reading of the man. 'Mr Lancaster's act impressed me a great deal. I strongly approved of suicide on principle, because I thought of it as an act of protest against society' (*DTV*, 54). The narrator dimly perceives that Lancaster, far from being a Mortmere grotesque, was a suffering human being. But it is the present-day, middle-aged 'Isherwood' – who introduces each section and provides retrospective commentary – who points out that

Lancaster's invitation was a belated plea for human contact. 'But of course it was already much too late,' he writes. 'He had lived too long inside his sounding box, listening to his own reverberations, his epic song of himself' (*DTV*, 56).

The next section is set on the Greek island of St Gregory, and was inspired by Isherwood's time on St Nicholas with Turville-Petre. The eponymous Ambrose is an alcoholic remittance man in flight from 'the others'. It transpires that he was at Cambridge with the narrator: on returning to his rooms one night, Ambrose discovers that the poshocracy has vandalized his engravings, china and marquetry writing desk. This incident is tantamount, Katherine Bucknell argues, to a 'gay-bashing'.[11] Utterly disillusioned by the experience, Ambrose quits Cambridge and spends the intervening years searching for a place in which he feels at home, and decides to buy St Gregory. The narrator conceives of Ambrose as 'one of Shakespeare's exiled kings', a Prospero figure biding his time before the homosexual revolution. 'Of course, when we do get into power,' Ambrose declares,

> we shall have to begin by reassuring everybody. We must make it clear that there'll be absolutely no reprisals. Actually, they'll be amazed to find how tolerant we are . . . I'm afraid we shan't be able to make heterosexuality actually legal, at first – there'd be too much of an outcry. One'll have to let at least twenty years go by, until all the resentment has died down. But meanwhile it'll be winked at, of course, as long as it's practiced in decent privacy. I think we shall even allow a few bars to be opened for people with those unfortunate tendencies, in certain quarters of the larger cities. (*DTV*, 103)

But St Gregory, far from being a gay paradise, turns out to be another hell. When the narrator apologizes for not recognizing Ambrose from Cambridge, Ambrose says it's understandable: 'After all, lovey, I'm dead and you aren't.' Geoffrey, another Cambridge exile, who cannot return to England after stealing money from the family business, ironically refers to 'our charming little Devil's Island'

and later characterizes it as 'utter hell' (*DTV*, 81, 101).[12] After the narrator has left St Gregory, he catches his reflection in a hotel mirror and glimpses a demon: 'My hair was long and matted, my beard had started to grow, I was sunburned nearly black . . . and my eyes were red' (*DTV*, 142).

At first, the narrator feels solidarity with Ambrose and Geoffrey, for he, too, has turned his back on England and the others. During his time in Berlin, he thought of himself as being part of the political struggle against the Nazis, but he now perceives that he was never 'a real partisan; only an excited spectator' (*DTV*, 68). He has come to St Gregory with Waldemar, with whom he reconnected in Berlin. 'Waldemar and I had developed an intimate but casual relationship which was typical of that period of my life. I knew at least half a dozen young men in much the same way' (*DTV*, 60). In reality, for Isherwood, this meant a sexual connection, but in *Down There* the namesake narrator is supposedly heterosexual. In *Christopher and His Kind*, Isherwood denied that Waldemar was based on Heinz, who accompanied him to St Nicholas: 'he is a mere second edition of the character of Otto Nowak. "Isherwood" treats Waldemar very much as he treats Otto in *Goodbye to Berlin*, with condescending amusement and without any suggestion that they are seriously involved' (*CK*, 143). Thus the 'love' the namesake narrator professes for Waldemar is presumably platonic, and he's unperturbed when Waldemar leaves the island. Although 'Isherwood' imagines that he is an outsider, when Ambrose suggests that he doesn't belong among the shades of St Gregory, he returns to England, thereby demonstrating that he was always a voluntary exile.

In 'Waldemar', the narrator is bound for England after a stint as a war reporter in China. As his steamer approaches Dover harbour, he runs into Dorothy, a devout communist he had known in Berlin with a bad case of 'worker worship', who, he learns, is now engaged to Waldemar. Because the narrator is ostensibly heterosexual, Dorothy is made to suffer the humiliation Isherwood endured at the hands of the immigration officials with Heinz. But the scene with Dorothy and Waldemar is less dramatic because they are part of the heterosexual majority, and Waldemar is given a temporary resident's permit rather than being expelled.

This section is the weakest in the novel. First, the titular character is Waldemar, but the private hell depicted seems to be the narrator's as he waits for the outcome of the negotiations between Hitler and Chamberlain. Second, unlike the sustained character portraits of Lancaster and Ambrose in the previous sections, Waldemar is only an intermittent presence in his section, which is largely composed of the narrator's diary entries and contains verbatim chunks of Isherwood's actual diary entries from the period.[13] Much like Kathleen, Dorothy's family disapprove of Waldemar and treat him like a servant; but when Dorothy proposes that they emigrate to Ecuador, Waldemar breaks off their engagement and voluntarily returns to Germany, which lacks the pathos of Heinz's arrest by the Gestapo. Third, the characterization in this section is often perfunctory: for example, there are a couple of references to a communist friend called Mary, but the narrator does not indicate how he knows her, or whether this is perhaps Mary Scriven from *The Memorial* and *The World in the Evening*, who was inspired by Olive Mangeot.[14] The same is true of the shadowy character of Dr Fisch, who seems to be the same person as the pipe-smoking dialectical materialist Katz in *The Condor and the Cows* and fulfils the same function as 'D.' in *Goodbye to Berlin*.[15] The brief appearances of Weston and Savage amount to little more than celebrity cameos, and whatever substance they possess is inherited from Isherwood's portraits of them in *Lions and Shadows*.

In the final section, Paul is a jaded male prostitute, who is intrigued when he learns that the narrator is involved with the guru Augustus Parr (who was modelled on Gerald Heard). Paul confesses that he's sick of sex and has been impotent for the past three months, and since sex is apparently the only thing he's good for, he resolves to kill himself. The narrator takes him to see Parr, who speaks of the necessity of making contact with 'this thing that's inside us and yet isn't us', in other words, the *atman* (*DTV*, 223). Paul agrees to meditate with Parr, and afterwards he recounts his life of 'greed and fear', which reminds Parr of the *Inferno*.

Paul moves in with the narrator, and together they pursue the contemplative life, as Isherwood had done with Denny Fouts. They participate in a spiritual retreat at Eureka Beach with some Quakers and Christians, which was based on the La Verne Seminar, and Isherwood reproduces some of his actual diary entries from this time. Paul has by now recovered his libido and engages in a flirtation with one of the daughters, the twelve-year-old Dee-Ann. The present-day narrator confides that a small part of himself was actively conniving in Paul's seduction of Dee-Ann, knowing that it would 'precipitate a scandal in which everything – the entire life I had been leading – would come to an end' (*DTV*, 300). When Dee-Ann's sister Alanna reports seeing Paul and Dee-Ann in flagrante, everyone assumes that it's true, and Paul is banished from the group, when in fact Alanna made it up because she was jealous. Despite his innocence, Paul makes no attempt to defend himself because he is weary of the spiritual path, and is sent to a forestry camp for conscientious objectors. With Paul gone, the narrator chooses the active over the contemplative life, and takes a job at a Quaker hostel for refugees.

If 'Paul' had ended at this point, it would have been more consistent with the previous sections, which were focused on a specific time and place. But the final section covers thirteen years and sprawls from Los Angeles to Paris and Berlin. Structurally, an epilogue that completed the stories of Paul and Waldemar would have made the novel more symmetrical, but Isherwood never considered this. Twelve years later, the narrator finds Paul living in Paris. Like Fouts, Paul is now an opium addict; when 'Isherwood' asks if he can try it, Paul is contemptuous: 'You're exactly like a tourist who thinks he can take in the whole of Rome in one day. You know, you really are a tourist, to your bones. I bet you're always sending post cards with "Down here on a visit" on them. That's the story of your life' (*DTV*, 344). Although Paul subsequently quits opium, he dies the following year during a party (presumably of a heart attack).

Down There was published in March 1962, and Isherwood was dismayed by the reviews. Several critics objected to the candid treatment of homosexuality. For instance, the reviewer in the American magazine *Commentary* complained: 'Every character seems to be either an Englishman or a homosexual – and for a while it makes little difference which.'[16] The prudish reviewer of the *Oxford Times* warned potential readers of the 'nauseating reek of homosexuality as one is led from one unhealthy circle to another'.[17] But these negative reviews would only spur Isherwood on to a more sustained attack on the heterosexual 'others' in *A Single Man*.

His relationship with Bachardy was becoming precarious. Don now wanted him to vacate Adelaide Drive in order to spend some time alone. Although Isherwood was keen to push on with the new novel he'd begun in March (provisionally titled *The Englishwoman*) and the Ramakrishna biography, he put out feelers for a teaching job in San Francisco and a lecture tour of Australia. Part of the problem was that Bachardy wanted to find a new style, in a new medium (paint), which allowed him to express himself in his portraits of others, and he displaced his creative frustration onto his relationship with Isherwood. At the same time, Isherwood was contending with a recrudescence of the gastric problems caused by his vagus nerve, and there was a spate of fatal cancers in his social circle, which led him to suspect that the burning sensation he now experienced on his tongue was cancer.

After completing the first 56 pages of his new novel, he felt unsure of its direction. 'I want to write about middle age, and being an alien. And about the Young' (*D2*, 221). He discussed it with Bachardy, who suggested that it should be called *The Englishman* and explore Isherwood's own experience of middle-aged alienation rather than that of his eponymous Englishwoman. That August Isherwood read *Mrs Dalloway* (1925) for the first time, and judged it 'one of the most truly beautiful novels . . . that I have ever read' (*D2*, 217).[18] He was struck by the elegance and efficacy of Woolf's interior monologues, and favourably compared them to Joyce's stream of consciousness technique, which had so impressed him as a young writer. This emboldened him to write what would become *A Single Man* in the third person, which he hadn't attempted since *The Memorial*.

He developed a godlike 'sub specie aeternitatis' voice,[19] 'which observes [the protagonist] like a wild creature, an antelope, with his daily habits and his whole symbolic meaning as a type' (*D2*, 245). He also borrowed the one-day circadian structure from *Mrs Dalloway*. The new novel seemed 'almost infinitely promising', and he affirmed: 'it is a possible *form* for a masterpiece, if only I could write it like a master!' (*D2*, 241).

Around this time, Bachardy began an affair with a friend named Bill Bopp, which persisted for a couple of months. Just when the 'Bill Bopp situation' seemed to have run its course, it was replaced by the 'Henry Kraft situation', with Bachardy insisting that Isherwood socialize with him.[20] Isherwood found the situation insufferable and predicted 'it is possible we might have parted by the summer' (*D2*, 269). Perhaps understandably, there was a marked uptick in Isherwood's drinking – or at any rate, there was an uptick in the accidents incurred by his drinking: in January 1963 he fell down at a party in Santa Barbara and cracked a rib; a few months later he 'sideswiped' a neighbour's car while driving home drunk; and in August he had another (presumably drunken) car crash, this time breaking a rib.

By July 1963 Isherwood had finished a second draft of *A Single Man* (Bachardy had suggested the new title). He showed it to Gavin Lambert, an expatriate friend and fellow novelist, who praised the novel but felt that the protagonist's 'way of speaking and his attitude to his college job are so absolutely me that one cannot accept him as an independent character' (*D2*, 283). But rather than adulterate the character by adding unconvincing extras to make him less like his author, as Isherwood had done with Stephen Monk in *The World in the Evening*, he wisely decided to leave George intact. He completed his final draft in October and sent it off to Methuen and Simon & Schuster. He had also been grinding out the final chapters of *Ramakrishna and His Disciples* (1965), describing it as 'the longest and cruellest of all my Vedanta chores' (*D2*, 289).

Despite the karmic boon of having completed the book, he capitulated to Prabhavananda's request to participate in the centenary celebrations of Vivekananda's birth, which would culminate in a Parliament of Religions in Calcutta (though perhaps the ongoing 'Henry Kraft situation' also played a part). Although Isherwood was now in the habit of making *japam* every day, he did it mechanically, without devotion, while his mind was preoccupied with secular matters. 'I still believe,' he wrote somewhat desperately in his diary. 'I still know that this is all that matters. And yet –' (*D*2, 291). He still pestered his guru with ingenuous questions, such as: 'You're really certain that God exists?' And: 'do you feel He gives you strength to bear misfortunes?' (*D*2, 133). Isherwood was therefore dreading the trip to India in December, and was braced for a psychosomatic showdown. A few days prior to his flight, he swallowed part of his dental plate while eating an ice cream and inferred that this was an unconscious (and, as it turned out, unsuccessful) bid to induce appendicitis.

He arrived at the headquarters of the Ramakrishna Mission at Belur Math, West Bengal, on 21 December. In addition to the numerous tributes to Vivekananda, two American devotees were to take *sannyas*, the second of two vows of renunciation required to become a fully fledged swami. One of them, John Yale, had begun his monastic training after reading Prabhavananda and Isherwood's translation of the *Gita* in 1948. Yale became the editor of *Vedanta and the West*, and helped to serialize Isherwood's biography of Ramakrishna; despite taking his *bramacharya* (chastity) vow in 1955, he was tormented with lust, and the situation was hardly helped when Isherwood lent him John Rechy's novel *City of Night* (1963), a sexually explicit story of a gay hustler. At the climax of the celebrations, Yale undertook the *sannyas* ceremony, having shaved his head and fasted (symbolic acts of renunciation), and became Swami Vidyatmananda. The following day, Isherwood prostrated before him and took the dust from his feet (an act of obeisance known as a *pranam*). It is possible that Yale, as a homosexual who had adhered to the monastic path and, for all his lustful thoughts, had succeeded in leading a celibate life and become a swami, represented for Isherwood a phantom self. At any rate, the experience of Yale's taking *sannyas* inspired Isherwood with the idea for his final novel, *A Meeting by the River* (1967).

At the end of December Isherwood was driven to Calcutta for the Parliament of Religions. There were around 8,000 people crammed into a marquee for the inaugural session, which lasted for three hours. Isherwood complained that the speakers mumbled their pious speeches, and estimated that only 1 per cent of the audience understood English. While anxious to get back to Bachardy in America and irritable at eating meals with his hands, he was still delivering his speeches with the appearance of good grace. But that evening he was stricken with diarrhoea, and as he lay awake in bed all his suppressed resentment regarding India and Prabhavananda came to a head. 'I resolved to tell him', wrote Isherwood,

> that I refuse ever again to appear in the temple or anywhere else and talk about God . . . As long as I quite unashamedly get drunk,

Group shot outside the Hollywood Temple at Ivar Avenue, *c.* 1952–3, including Christopher Isherwood (standing in the middle, wearing a tie), John Yale (to Isherwood's left, with arms crossed), Swami Prabhavananda (seated in front of Isherwood and Yale) and Gerald Heard (to Prabhavananda's left).

have sex and write books like *A Single Man*, I simply cannot appear before people as a sort of lay minister . . . For me, religion must be quite private as far as I'm publicly concerned. I can still write about it *informatively*, but I must not appear before people on a platform as a living witness and example. (*D*2, 319)

Isherwood was feeling somewhat better on New Year's Day, and decided to give his speech as planned about Girish Ghosh, a dissolute dramatist, actor and womanizer, who was converted by Ramakrishna. Isherwood had been inspired by Ghosh's story because Ramakrishna, much like Prabhavananda, did not condemn Ghosh for his drunkenness and sexual appetite, but rather recognized in his vices a misplaced longing for transcendence. Ramakrishna would stop his carriage in the street and dance with drunkards, Isherwood pointed out: 'Well,' Ramakrishna would reflect, 'this is really exactly the same as ecstasy. It is only that he is going about it the wrong way.'[21] This speech puts his private rant above into perspective: Isherwood was speaking, not as a swami on the importance of continence, but as the biographer of Ramakrishna who identified with Ghosh, who looked for ecstasy in the wrong places. The next day, though, his illness returned, and he vented his spleen on Prabhavananda. 'I've made up my mind,' he told him: 'I can't ever talk about God and religion in public again . . . I feel like a prostitute. I've felt like that after all of these meetings of the parliament, when I've spoken' (*D*2, 325).

While Isherwood was away, Auden had confided to Bachardy that he felt Isherwood disliked his partner Chester Kallman because he was Jewish. On the one hand, there's no denying that Isherwood was deeply antisemitic. He unblushingly deployed pejorative nouns like 'Jewboy' and used the word 'jew' as a verb – for example, he complained that Berkeley had 'tried to jew me down to some ridiculous and impudent offer' (*D*2, 191). He objected to the casting of the gentile Montgomery Clift as the Jewish Sigmund Freud in John Huston's biopic: 'It is the most bogus kind of liberal nonsense', he wrote, 'that we're all the same really. We fucking well aren't' (*D*2, 218). On the other hand, he had several Jewish friends, such as

Stephen Spender and Berthold Viertel, and his dislike for Kallman chiefly derived from his character.[22] Moreover, he was always territorial about Auden and resented Kallman's claims on his attention (and doubtless Auden felt the same way about Bachardy).

In February 1964 Auden telegraphed Isherwood to inform him that *A Single Man* was his best book. The novel charts a day in the life of George, a middle-aged English professor who is mourning the death of his lover Jim, from the moment he wakes to the moment he loses consciousness (or, debatably, dies) that night. Although the novel was now tightly focused on George, rather than his friend and fellow expatriate Charlotte (the original protagonist of *The Englishwoman*), Isherwood's choice of an omniscient third-person narrator allows him to supply a Vedantic framework, without having to introduce a guru figure like Augustus Parr, or worse, having George somehow intuit Vedantic insights from his experience like Stephen Monk in *The World in the Evening*. 'Waking up begins with saying *am* and *now*. That which has awoken then lies for a while staring up at the ceiling and down into itself until it has recognised *I*, and therefrom deduced *I am, I am now*. *Here* comes next, and is at least negatively reassuring; because *here*' is 'what's called *at home*' (SM, 1).

The key teachings of Advaita Vedanta derive from the Upanishads. The *Mandukya Upanishad* outlines four states of being: waking, dreaming, deep sleep and *turiya* (pure consciousness or *samadhi*). The first two states are dualistic, divided between seer (subject) and seen (the objects of the world or, in dreams, the imagination), but this distinction disappears in the third.[23] 'The condition of deep sleep is one of oneness, a mass of silent consciousness made of peace and enjoying peace.'[24] The negative non-duality of deep sleep offers a 'foretaste' of the positive unity of *samadhi*, in which state one realizes that one's true self or *atman* is no different from *brahman*; this is one reason why deep sleep is so restorative.[25] Thus on re-entering the dualistic waking state, it takes some moments for the illusion of George's ego to coalesce in time ('*I am now*') and space ('*here*').

George may have a different name but he is the same age and weight as Isherwood, and his body shares the same ailments, such as 'arthritic thumbs' and problems with his 'vagus nerve'. After making his ablutions: 'It knows its name. It is called George' (*SM*, 3). It is only when George enters the kitchen that his grief returns: 'It is here that he stops short and knows, with a sick newness, almost as though it were for the first time: Jim is dead. Is dead' (*SM*, 3). The title, then, reflects George's loneliness after Jim's death, but it also signifies his profound psychological isolation. While moving his bowels (an allusion to Leopold Bloom and that other, famously circadian, novel *Ulysses*), George reflects on his pariah status among his neighbours. He is the lone queer in their heterosexual paradise of married couples, barbecues and raucous children (who torment him by playing on his property). He finds the tolerance of his neighbour Mrs Strunk towards his sexuality even more intolerable than her husband's homophobia: 'All is due to heredity, early environment (shame on those possessive mothers, those sex-segregated British schools!), arrested development at puberty, and/or glands' (*SM*, 16). Thus George has not told the neighbours of Jim's death, and pretends that Jim has moved back east to take care of his parents, for he cannot expect them to comprehend his grief. Likewise, he did not interact with Jim's family after his death and refused to go to the funeral.

But his neighbours are merely a microcosm of the larger enemy – namely, the others. On his drive to San Tomas State College, George fantasizes about commanding an army of assassins who will reap revenge on the war-mongering senators, homophobic newspaper editors and greedy developers who infuriate him:

> All are, in the last analysis, responsible for Jim's death . . . But, when George gets in as deep as this, Jim hardly matters any more. Jim is nothing, now, but an excuse for hating three quarters of the population of America . . . Rage, resentment, spleen; of such is the vitality of middle age. (*SM*, 26)

The only people with whom George sympathizes are the members of other minority groups, such as the poor Mexicans and African

Americans who live in the tract housing beyond the college campus. In his seminar on *After Many a Summer*, George gets into a discussion about minorities: 'a minority is only thought of as a minority when it constitutes some kind of a threat to the majority, real or imaginary.' He rejects the liberal orthodoxy that everyone is the same. 'But, the worst of it is,' he adds, 'we now run into another liberal heresy. Because the persecuting majority is vile, says the liberal, therefore the persecuted minority must be stainlessly pure. Can't you see what nonsense that is?' (SM, 54). Isherwood counteracts this tendency in his depiction of George, who, far from being a homosexual saint, is a flawed, peccant and hence recognizable human being.

After teaching his class, George visits a friend called Doris, who is dying in hospital. At some point in the past, Doris had seduced Jim, but looking at her body now, which appears like a 'yellow shrivelled manikin with its sticks of arms and legs', he can no longer summon up the old anger and resentment. 'As long as one tiny precious drop of hate remained, George could still find something left in her of Jim,' writes the narrator. 'That has been the bond between him and Doris. And now it is broken. And one more bit of Jim is lost to him for ever' (SM, 81). On leaving the hospital, he rejoices that he is part of that other minority – the living: '*I am alive*, he says to himself, *I am alive!* And life-energy surges hotly through him, and delight, and appetite. How good to be in a body – even this old beat-up carcase – that still has warm blood and live semen and rich marrow and wholesome flesh!' (SM, 82)

Unable to face eating alone, George arranges to have dinner with his friend Charlotte, the only person with whom he has shared his grief. At the end of the Second World War, Charlotte married a G.I., moved to the United States and had a son; but the marriage didn't last and now her son accuses her of 'smother[ing] him' and wants a 'complete break'. In her cups, Charlotte waxes nostalgic about England, which she associates with the past, and contemplates returning there to live with her sister. 'The Past is over,' George informs her. 'People make believe that it isn't, and they show you things in museums. But that's not the Past. You won't find the Past in England. Or anywhere else, for that matter' (*SM*, 113–14).

In a drunken *carpe diem* impulse on the way home, George decides to visit a local bar near the beach where he first met Jim. There he encounters one of his students, Kenny, who, despite having a Japanese girlfriend, seems to be intent on getting to know George better. After several scotches, they decide to go skinny dipping. George's swim is presented in terms of rebirth: 'Then, intent upon his own rites of purification, George staggers out once more, wide-open-armed, to receive the stunning baptism of the surf. Giving himself to it utterly, he washes away thought, speech, mood, desire, whole selves, entire lifetimes; again and again he returns, becoming always cleaner, freer, less' (*SM*, 132).

Back at George's house, Kenny has a shower and George gives him a blanket to cover himself while his clothes dry, which the narrator likens to a 'chlamys', the 'classical Greek garment . . . worn by a young [philosopher's] disciple' (*SM*, 138). (Earlier, in the bar, George fondly imagines their drunken conversation as a 'Platonic dialogue', and Isherwood seems to be alluding to the 'classical' – that is, pederastic – relationship that obtained in ancient Greece between adult men and teenaged boys.) George is by now very drunk and delivers a fervent only-connect speech:

> It's the enormous tragedy of everything nowadays. Flirtation. Flirtation instead of fucking, if you'll pardon my coarseness. All any of you ever do is flirt, and wear your blankets off one shoulder . . . And miss the one thing that might really – and, Kenneth, I do not say this casually – *transform your entire life*. (*SM*, 144)

But George passes out before anything can happen, and he wakes sometime later to discover that Kenny has put him to bed in his pyjamas, leaving a note that does not clarify whether his interest in George is sexual or intellectual.

After masturbating, George falls asleep again: 'the brain inside its skull on the pillow cognises darkly' and 'can become aware, in this state, of certain decisions apparently not yet made' (*SM*, 148). According to the *Mandukya Upanishad*, the 'silent consciousness' of deep sleep is 'all-knowing',[26] and so it's possible that George is permitted an unconscious glimpse of the future:

> *Will George go back to England?*
> No. He will stay here.
> *Because of Jim?*
> No. Jim is in the Past, now. He is of no use to George, any more.
> *But George remembers him so faithfully.*
> George makes himself remember. He is afraid of forgetting. Jim is my life, he says. But he will have to forget, if he wants to go on living. Jim is Death. (*SM*, 148–9)

George's journey on this day can be encapsulated in the statements 'Jim is dead' in the morning to the night-time realization that 'Jim is Death.'[27] In order to heal, George must let go of the past, with its memories of Jim, and embrace the present. 'It is Now that he must find another Jim. Now that he must love. Now that he must live' (*SM*, 149). But this message is often obfuscated by the novel's coda, in which the narrator likens the artificial entity of George's ego to a 'rock pool', whose creatures are akin to the darting thoughts, emotions and impulses 'George' experiences. During the day, the rock pool is isolated from the ocean by the ebb tide. 'But that long day ends at last,' notes the narrator:

> yields to the night-time of the flood. And, just as the waters of the ocean come flooding, darkening over the pools, so over George and the others in sleep come the waters of that other ocean; that consciousness which is no one in particular but which contains everyone and everything, past, present and future, and extends unbroken beyond the uttermost stars. We may surely suppose that, in the darkness of the full flood, some of these creatures are lifted from their pools to drift far out over the deep waters. But do they ever bring back, when the daytime of the ebb returns, any kind of catch with them?

> Can they tell us, in any manner, about their journey? Is there, indeed, anything for them to tell – except that the waters of the ocean are not really other than the waters of the pool? (*SM*, 150)

The metaphor conveys the individual's experience of non-duality in deep sleep, in which the distinction between subject and object, rock pool and ocean, disappears. But this does not mean that George will awake from sleep with the mystical conviction that *atman* and *brahman* are one – after all, the night before the narrative begins, George also experienced the non-duality of deep sleep, but he awoke to his old hatreds and resentments. If George's intuition of the future is anything to go by, he will wake and pursue mundane happiness in the present in the form of 'another Jim', rather than retiring to the cloister. The narrator then complicates matters by *supposing* that 'plaque' has been gradually accumulating in George's coronary artery and will result in a fatal heart attack:

> And if some part of the non-entity we called George has indeed been absent at this moment of terminal shock, away out there on the deep waters, then it will return to find itself homeless. For it can associate no longer with what lies here, unsnoring, on the bed. This is now cousin to the garbage in the container on the back porch. Both will have to be carted away and disposed of, before too long. (*SM*, 152)

The critic Claude Summers has asserted that: 'In death, George's spirit will merge with the universal consciousness.'[28] Possibly this is the conclusion Isherwood intended, but it does not conform to a Vedantic worldview, in which only those people who have experienced enlightenment in life will achieve liberation; for agnostics like George, their *purusha* will be reborn in accordance with their karma in another body. Paul Piazza notes that George is ignorant of the 'mystical ramifications' of the narrative, and that his day constitutes a spiritual allegory that can only be appreciated by the reader.[29]

Alas, the spiritual dimension of the novel was almost wholly lost on Isherwood's peers. John Gross, writing in the *New Statesman*, summed up the novel thus: 'And one day soon – who knows, perhaps tonight – [George] is going to fall asleep and never wake up.'[30] The most offensive review came from the *Los Angeles Times* under the homophobic tagline 'Disjointed Limp Wrist Saga': 'All this defense mechanism built up for the homosexual is, of course, disgusting. But the tasteless fatuity of the book is its most unfortunate aspect.' The protagonist 'lives in a gamy half-world of student titterings, resentment against growing old, anger at a world that refuses him a perverted lebensraum – rattling the tin cup of his despair against the bars of his peculiar practices'.[31] Despite what Isherwood described as the 'sour reception' of *A Single Man* in America, he regarded it as his masterpiece: 'I spoke the truth, and now let them swallow it or not as they see fit. That's a very good feeling, and this is the first time that I have really felt it' (*D*2, 341).

7
Life Writing, 1965–80

Isherwood began his last novel, *A Meeting by the River*, in the spring of 1965. As usual, he plunged into the book impetuously, without bothering to make a plan, and got stuck after 25 pages. At this stage, all he knew was that the novel was about two brothers: the worldly Patrick and the world-denying Oliver, who is about to take *sannyas* in an Indian monastery. The narrative would build towards a confrontation, with Patrick urging Oliver not to become a swami, which would not only illustrate their contrasting personalities but alter both their lives in some way. He subsequently decided that while his central story was fine, the approach was wrong: the narrative would now proceed through letters and diary entries. By June he had finished a first draft, but was dissatisfied with it.

Although he was writing his most explicitly religious novel, his faith was at a low ebb. 'Spent a little time in the temple' at Ivar Avenue, he wrote in March 1966, 'but all the lines seem to be disconnected'. On entering Prabhavananda's room, 'I said to myself, I am going to visit a saint . . . but I couldn't feel it' (*D2*, 389). Isherwood's position had always been that if he sometimes found it hard to believe in the reality of *brahman* (steeped as he was in *maya*), he knew a man who did, and that he had faith in Prabhavananda's faith, but even this was wavering. He completed his third draft of *A Meeting by the River* at the end of May. Given the novel's Indian setting and Vedanta philosophy, he knew he'd have to give the manuscript to Prabhavananda, and felt abashed by the prospect of his reading the scenes involving

Patrick and his lover Tom. He needn't have worried, though: Prabhavananda wept at the ending and suggested that the novel be stocked in the Vedanta Center bookshop.

A Meeting by the River was published by Methuen in June 1967. Since becoming Prabhavananda's disciple in 1940, all Isherwood's books had been inflected with Vedanta philosophy, but *A Meeting by the River* is the only novel that overtly employs Hindu concepts and vocabulary, whereas in his previous work the religious characters tended to be Quakers and he'd relied on metaphors (such as the rock pool and the ocean) to convey Vedantic ideas. *A Meeting by the River* is set in a Hindu monastery on the banks of the Ganges, near Calcutta. It tells the story of two brothers: the secular Patrick, who publishes titillating showbiz memoirs and is now producing a film; and the monastic Oliver, who worked with the Quakers and the Red Cross, until he met a Vedanta swami and became his disciple. When the novel opens in 1964, Oliver is preparing to take his *sannyas* vows, after which he will become a swami and be given a Sanskrit name (which symbolizes spiritual rebirth). The novel is composed of Oliver's diary and the letters Patrick writes to his brother, his mother, his patient wife Penelope (Isherwood was obviously thinking of the *Odyssey*) and his lover Tom in Los Angeles.

Patrick is cast as a suave Satan figure to Oliver's saint, who comes to the monastery on the pretext of brotherly love, but whose aim is to stop Oliver from taking his vows by tempting him with worldly pleasure and power. Isherwood underlines the symbolism: 'I sometimes feel slightly Satanic,' writes Patrick, after telling Oliver how he has 'corrupted' his partners by convincing them to publish the prurient memoirs that are his speciality and getting them to invest in his film (*MR*, 21). He invites Oliver into his room while he is exercising naked, causing Oliver to pay attention to 'his rather big penis' (*MR*, 61).[1] One of Isherwood's original ideas for the novel was to make Patrick and Oliver half-brothers, and to have Patrick seduce his brother when they were growing up, which would render Oliver ashamed of his homosexuality and attracted to celibacy.[2] Although Isherwood abandoned this idea, there remains a strange incestuous connection between the brothers. In his diary, Oliver confesses that he fell in love with Penny partly because she was Patrick's fiancée. 'When I was going through my Freudian phase,' he recalls, 'I used to wonder if I wasn't actually in love with [Patrick], romantically and even physically. I'm quite sure now that that's not true, at least not any longer' (*MR*, 104). As for Patrick, he has an erotic dream he refers to as a 'vision', in which Tom is the idealized 'brother' for whom he has been searching. It's worth recalling that Isherwood often regarded himself as an 'elder brother' to his younger lovers, such as Heinz; Patrick, who in his late thirties is about two decades older than Tom, seems to fulfil the same role.

The epistolary format of the novel allows Isherwood to expose Patrick's dishonesty and guile. To his mother he reports that Oliver is quite happy at the monastery despite never marrying and having children like himself, flagging up the fact that he (rather than Oliver) has fulfilled his filial duty. He subtly represents Oliver's decision to become a monk as selfish: 'And isn't it refreshing, in these days of conformity, to know of one human being at least who always seems to do exactly what he wants to do, not what he has to do?' (*MR*, 32). He writes to Penny that Oliver pressed him for details about her, when in fact he studiously avoided the subject, then leaves the letter out for Oliver to read it, perhaps hoping to stir up his brother's jealousy or resentment and thereby break the monastic mask. He urges Tom to be 'cunning' about their affair, and adds that he doesn't want to be a 'martyr' to the cause, 'because it might mean losing you', when it is his marriage and social standing that he's unwilling to sacrifice (*MR*, 78).

Much like Stephen Monk, part of Patrick's untrustworthiness derives from his bisexuality. In some lecture notes regarding his work, Isherwood wrote that he had tried to show that 'bisexuality has a deep untruthfulness, because, in our culture, it amounts to "passing"' (in the racial sense of the word).[3] Thus Patrick accrues the benefits of conformity on the one hand – marriage, children, security and so on – and the transgressive thrill of his homosexual affairs on the other. This is nowhere more apparent than in his dream 'vision' of Tom, where they live without fear and 'share everything together in the flesh and in the spirit', and yet at the same time he affirms 'that our being together is going to find its place and fit in amongst the other relationships of our lives, without even causing any great disturbance!' (*MR*, 121–2). But when Tom exceeds his impossible dream role by phoning the monastery and drunkenly professing his love to Oliver (mistaking him for Patrick), Patrick dumps him in a cowardly manner. To add insult to injury, Patrick urges Tom to get married and have children. And in his letter to Penny, he obliquely admits to cheating on her but has the effrontery to ask her permission to continue his affairs:

> I can promise you one thing, I shall always return from these idiotic adventures with increased love for you and gratitude – in fact, I can only enjoy the adventures if you'll sanction them! Oh Penny, can't we forget about 'marriage' altogether and live in our own special way, the way that's natural to us? Can't I quite shamelessly be the child who keeps running home to you, and who is always thinking of you even in the midst of his play? (*MR*, 173)

Thus Penny is cast in the role of mother, while his male lovers (Tom isn't the first) are represented as his brothers. On the one hand, Patrick's bisexual bad faith undermines the reader's sympathy; on the other, Isherwood has at least succeeded in creating a credible central character who isn't himself, in contrast to Stephen Monk.

The novel inexorably builds towards Oliver's dark night of the soul, in which he is beset by religious doubts and contemplates returning to England. The crisis is provoked by Patrick's assertion that Oliver has a rare leadership quality that is 'inseparable from ambition', but the idea of ambition is so repugnant he hides from it by undertaking charity work with the Quakers and Red Cross. According to Patrick, Oliver was attracted to his swami because he promised to 'annihilate' his 'ego and ambition' (*MR*, 144). After explaining away Oliver's religious convictions in psychological terms, Patrick offers to pull some strings and get him a job with the United Nations, where he can exercise his leadership skills with a good conscience. If Oliver is tempted by Patrick's offer, it is partly because he has a sort of vicarious faith in the manner of Isherwood: 'I have known a man who said *he knew* that God exists' (*MR*, 43).

After a sleepless night of soul searching, Oliver falls into a doze and has a vision of his swami, who has recently died. In his vision – a religious analogue to Patrick's secular vision of brotherhood with Tom – the swami reassures Oliver that Patrick, for all his spiritual disarray, will be saved, since he is now under the swami's protection. On waking, Oliver decides that Patrick wanted to persuade him not to become a monk because he was dissatisfied with his worldly life, and needed to assure himself that the spiritual path was false. Patrick's newfound dissatisfaction, Oliver believes, derives from his being unknowingly in a 'state of grace' due to the swami's influence. When Oliver emerges from the *sannyas* ceremony the following day at dawn, Patrick is there to meet him and performs a *pranam*, taking the dust from his feet. 'And everybody was smiling and murmuring,' writes Oliver, 'as much as to say how charming it was of Patrick to play this scene according to our local Hindu rules, and how very right and proper it was that we two brothers should love each other' (*MR*, 180).

In an interview, Isherwood affirmed that the novel had been criticized for its ambiguous ending, and that he had intended the reader to decide whether Oliver was right and that Patrick would be saved by dint of his association with the swami, or whether Patrick was right in his prediction to Penny that Oliver would ultimately channel his leadership skills by becoming an incorruptible eminence like Gandhi.[4] Predictably most critics, given the unwelcome spectacle of a candidly religious novel (and a Hindu one to boot), found themselves nostalgic for the atheist Herr Issyvoo.[5] The *TLS* reviewer found the book 'embarrassing', with its 'awkward combination of Vedantic piety and sexual frankness'. He concluded: 'If you blushed at *A Single Man* you will writhe at *A Meeting by the River*.'[6]

Meanwhile, Isherwood was enjoying a 'marvellous phase of love, intimacy, mutual trust, tenderness, affection, fun' with Bachardy (*D2*, 465). The days of Don's serious love affairs (such as the 'Henry Kraft situation') seemed to be behind them. But the following year Bachardy embarked on an affair that almost scuppered their relationship. He was bewitched by the theatre director Anthony Page while in London, and what was meant to be a short break turned into an absence of ten weeks. Bachardy eventually returned to Santa Monica in June 1968, but the affair with Page would persist, intermittently, for almost two years. One similarity with the 'Henry Kraft situation' was that Bachardy's affair with Page began during a period of artistic frustration. Wanting to keep Bachardy close and find a new outlet for his creativity, Isherwood asked him to collaborate on the stage version of *A Meeting by the River*. But the plan backfired, for the resulting script provided Bachardy with a pretext for returning to London, where they hoped to find a producer.

According to David Hockney, whom they'd met in 1964 and was now a close friend, Bachardy seriously contemplated leaving Isherwood for Page.[7] Hockney's painting *Christopher Isherwood and Don Bachardy* (1968), with a hawkish Isherwood in profile jealousy scrutinizing his partner, who sits in an armchair beside him but

Bachardy and Isherwood, February 1970, in front of David Hockney's double portrait *Christopher Isherwood and Don Bachardy*, 1968, acrylic on canvas.

ignores him, staring straight ahead, captures the asymmetry in their relationship. In the event, Page had scant desire to direct *A Meeting by the River*, infuriating Bachardy.[8] The script went through numerous revisions and passed through the hands of countless producers, actors and directors, but it was never performed in London; eventually, the screenwriter and director James Bridges, who'd initially suggested the project, put on a successful production in Los Angeles in 1972.

During this period, Isherwood had been working on a memoir of his parents, titled *Kathleen and Frank*, which was published by Methuen in October 1971. He had originally intended the book to be an exploration of Jungian myth-making in his work. Although Isherwood had been a keen student of Freud in the 1920s, he didn't read Jung until the mid-1960s. In a lecture from 1965, he quotes from *Memories, Dreams, Reflections* (1961):

> What we are to our inner vision . . . can only be expressed by way of myth . . . So it is that I have now undertaken . . . to tell my personal myth. I can only tell stories. Whether or not the stories are true is not the problem. The only question is whether what I tell is *my* fable, *my* truth.

In his notes, Isherwood added: 'Hence the novelist's distortion of experience. What really happened is not as "true" (i.e. not *his* truth) as what he makes happen. Writing is the exploration of one's myth, rather than one's experience.'[9] This was what Isherwood had been groping towards in his autofiction: the revelation of a deeper artistic truth through the fictionalization or mythologization of experience.

The most intriguing aspect of *Kathleen and Frank* is the elaborate mythos that emerged from Isherwood's relationship with his parents. The catalyst was his father's death in the Great War, which transformed Frank into the 'hero-father' while Kathleen was pressed into the part of the 'holy widow', whose unspeakable grief was an Oedipal outrage to her son, who was saddled with the role of 'sacred orphan'. These mythic roles were imposed by the avatars of the establishment he labelled 'the others', and his rebellion consisted in overturning the others' traditions and creating his own anti-myth. In place of the others' 'hero-father', he forged the 'anti-heroic hero' from cherished memories of Frank and his idiosyncrasies: in the Isherwood mythos, Frank is an artist at heart who mocks the military by wearing its uniform, who draws cartoons on army documents and knits while battles rage around him. The anti-heroic Frank maintains that he uses his sword for toasting bread and never draws his revolver because he is a terrible shot.

> He lives this masquerade right through, day by day to the end, and crowns his performance by actually getting himself killed in battle. By thus fooling everybody (except Christopher) into believing he is the Hero-Father, he demonstrates the absurdity of the military mystique and its solemn cult of War and Death. (*KF*, 503)

It's no coincidence that Isherwood was attracted to 'anti-heroic heroes' in his personal life, such as Gerald Hamilton, Berthold Viertel, Francis Turville-Petre and E. M. Forster, and that he felt compelled to write about them in his novels. As Brian Finney points out 'Mr Norris, Bergmann, Ambrose, and E. M.' are all 'paternalistic figures in secret revolt against the establishment'.[10]

Isherwood quotes two letters from Frank, written a few months prior to his death: 'I don't think it matters very much what Christopher learns as long as he remains himself and keeps his individuality and develops on his own lines,' he wrote in one; and in the other he hoped that St Edmund's wouldn't pasteurize Christopher's character: 'I for one would much rather have him as he is' (*KF*, 505). In retrospect, this validated Isherwood's choice to be a writer rather than a stockbroker or a don, and to spurn the conventional trajectory of marriage and children. Nonetheless, he acknowledged that if Frank had survived the war he would have been consternated by his son's homosexuality, his Marxist attitudinizing and his conversion to pacifism. 'It was more likely', he writes, 'that Frank would have forgotten he had ever wanted Christopher to "develop on his own lines"', and that 'he would have ended by disowning' him (*KF*, 506).

As for Kathleen, she became a 'demon-mother' because she upheld the values and traditions of the others. In his new role as 'anti-son', as opposed to 'sacred orphan', Isherwood contested her convictions and worldview: he became an atheist to mock her Christianity; in response to her unthinking love for Mother England, he embraced Germany, the fatherland that had killed Frank; he set his homosexuality against her conventional desire for grandchildren; when Kathleen suggested that he become an academic, he got himself sent down from Cambridge; he reviled Marple Hall and declared his wish to burn it down because Kathleen loved it as a sacred symbol of the past; he was immediately drawn to Edward Upward at Repton because of his towering hatred for everything Kathleen prized – public schools, the poshocracy, the establishment.

It was this 'demon-mother' archetype that Isherwood drew on when portraying Mrs Lindsay in *All the Conspirators* and Lily Vernon in *The Memorial*. In the former, Mrs Lindsay attempts to thwart her son's artistic ambitions and encourages him to stick with the respectable office job he finds anathema. In contrast to Philip Lindsay, Isherwood's literary ambitions clearly benefitted from the 'counterforce' of Kathleen's philistinism. As an adolescent, he was 'enraged' by Kathleen's use of the adjective 'soothing' to describe the middlebrow books she admired, and believed that it betrayed her 'subconscious contempt for all literature' (*KF*, 26). In response to Kathleen's snobbish ancestor-worship, he created 'a private aristocracy of the arts' that he peopled with 'his own peerage' (*KF*, 268). After dropping out of Cambridge, he refused to take a respectable teaching job and chose to become a secretary to a string quartet, beguiled by the bohemian atmosphere of the Mangeots' mews house in Kensington, in contrast to the stuffy propriety of Marple Hall. These two worlds were vividly evoked in *The Memorial*, with Mary Scriven representing the exuberant bohemia of Olive Mangeot, in which the living are given precedence over the dead, while Lily Vernon embodies Kathleen's cult of the past and hatred of the present.

Isherwood's détente with Kathleen occurred when, after almost twenty years, she stopped grieving and allowed herself to feel joy. By this time, his reputation as a writer had been ratified by good reviews and prestigious literary friends, and Kathleen now took a palpable pride in his career. On the one hand, his emigration to the United States in 1939 symbolized the ultimate separation of 'Mother and Motherland'; on the other hand, he affirmed that 'the days of his opposition to Kathleen were over' (*KF*, 509). As he got older, he recognized certain aspects of himself in Kathleen. To begin with, they were both inveterate diary writers. Furthermore, in America Isherwood's behaviour and beliefs were no longer antipathetic to Kathleen's. He embraced religion, becoming a Vedantin. Curiously, Frank had been a reluctant churchgoer and took an interest in Theosophy, which incorporated many Hindu doctrines.[11] In addition, Isherwood had become an academic by accepting temporary teaching posts at U.S. colleges. And by mythologizing his life in his diaries and fiction, he too had become 'a celebrant of the Past' (*KF*, 2).

Kathleen and Frank is largely told through his parents' letters and diaries, and he made a couple of trips to Wyberslegh while researching the book. Marple Hall had been demolished in 1959 and was now the site of Marple Hall Grammar School. All that remained of the building, when Isherwood visited in October 1966, was a keystone lying in the grass, dated 1658. 'Christopher felt wonderfully joyful,' he recalls in *Kathleen and Frank*. 'For him, this certainly wasn't the end of an ancient enemy but it did seem to be the lifting of a curse. Whatever here had exercised an evil power seemed appeased now and buried, like Heathcliff in Gimmerton churchyard' (*KF*, 330–31).

In his afterword, Isherwood confides that while researching the book he perceived 'how heredity and kinship create a woven fabric' and that ultimately it's hard to ascertain 'exactly where Kathleen and Frank end and Richard and Christopher begin' (*KF*, 510). As soon as he began to read Kathleen's diaries, he was filled with regret that he hadn't been gracious enough to read them in her lifetime; Kathleen had forlornly remarked to Richard, referring to her diaries:

'perhaps someone will be glad of it, some day' (*KF*, 3). *Kathleen and Frank*, then, is at once an expiation of this oversight and can be read as a counter-narrative to the demon-mothers, hero-fathers and anti-heroic heroes that haunt his fiction. He quotes a diary entry from 1909, in which Kathleen notes that the five-year-old Isherwood 'dictated a story called *The Adventures of Mummy and Daddy*', which was 'chiefly about himself'. Despite the title, *Kathleen and Frank* is an excavation of the Isherwood mythos and, as such, much like *The Adventures of Mummy and Daddy*, it is 'chiefly about Christopher' (*KF*, 349, 511).

Now that Bachardy had finished his affair with Page, their relationship was stronger than ever. But Isherwood's happiness was increasingly undermined by the spectre of his death. Both Forster and Gerald Hamilton had died in June 1970. Gerald Heard, who had suffered over twenty strokes which impaired his speech and finally left him comatose, died in August 1971. For several years, Isherwood had been praying to Ramakrishna for 'help in the hour of death', and in addition to making *japam* he was now meditating in the mornings and trying to practise recollection (an awareness or mindfulness of *brahman*). Furthermore Auden, who was two and half years his junior, died of a heart attack at the end of September 1973. Reading through Auden's correspondence in the wake of his death, Isherwood reproached himself for being the negligent partner in their friendship: 'He loved me very much and I behaved rather badly to him, a lot of the time. Again and again, in the later letters, he begs me to come and spend some time alone with him. Why didn't I?' (*D3*, 402).

Around this time, Isherwood began a new book, tentatively titled *Wanderings*, which would be an odyssey of his early years in America. It was meant to start with Auden and himself departing for New York in 1939, but he was unable to make any progress. Eventually he realized that he needed to contextualize his emigration to America by including his sexual adventures in Germany and his European wanderings with Heinz. This material was supposed to serve as a prologue to the main American narrative, but a hundred pages later he had only reached 1935. He found the Berlin years particularly vexatious because he had written so vividly about Gerald Hamilton, Jean Ross, Frl. Thurau and others in *Mr Norris* and *Goodbye to Berlin*. Indeed, reading through his earlier work he was struck by its 'ease and brightness' and worried that his late style was 'ponderous' in comparison. 'But how deeply all this interests me! I don't think I have ever felt so challenged and turned on by any other project' (*D3*, 408). After another hundred pages, he had brought the narrative up to 1939, and was contemplating publishing the book in two volumes, but rather than push on with the American section, he immediately began to revise what he had done, and little by little he abandoned the idea of a second volume and published the book as *Christopher and His Kind*.

Isherwood begins the book by disparaging his previous autobiography, *Lions and Shadows*, for being disingenuous, for concealing 'important facts' about himself, falsely dramatizing his experience and using 'fictitious names' for his friends. In contrast, *Christopher and His Kind* will be unremittingly honest, 'especially as far as I myself am concerned' (*CK*, 1). But the idea that *Lions and Shadows* is subjective and fictional while *Christopher and His Kind* is wholly objective does not bear scrutiny. For a start, Isherwood does use some fictitious names in *Christopher and His Kind*: he uses the name Vernon for his first American boyfriend (Harvey Young); Stephen Spender's partner Tony Hyndman is given the *nom de guerre* Jimmy Younger (this name is borrowed from Spender's memoir *World within World*); he refers to Walter Wolff by his fictional name Otto Nowak; and finally, Heinz Neddermeyer and Francis Turville-Petre are denoted only by their first names. Furthermore, the book is structured like a novel, with scenes and dialogue Isherwood couldn't possibly have remembered forty years later. For example, the interview with Heinz and the immigration officials at Harwich reads like a dramatic set-piece. When asked in an interview about the book's structure, Isherwood stated: 'If *Christopher and His Kind* does in fact read like a novel, perhaps it's because I've always felt very little difference between fiction and fact.'[12] In other words, *Christopher and His Kind* is a work of autofiction and not, as he maintained in his diary, a 'true autobiography' (*D3*, 408).

Isherwood and W. H. Auden, 6 February 1939, by Carl van Vechten.

The book begins where *Lions and Shadows* left off, with Isherwood on the train to Berlin in March 1929. As an avatar for the gay liberation movement, who spoke at queer conferences and events, he was eager to make amends for the circumspect treatment of homosexuality in his early work by describing his sex life in Berlin. He reprises the reasons he'd given in his lecture 'The Autobiography of My Books' for concealing the sexuality of William Bradshaw and

Herr Issyvoo, namely that he wanted the reader to focus on Mr Norris, Sally Bowles, Otto Nowak and Natalia Landauer rather than his narrator.[13] By eliding the sexuality of Herr Issyvoo, the phrase 'I am a camera' became a trope for Isherwood the 'eternal outsider' who watches 'the passing parade of life . . . with wistful impotence'. After quoting from the opening of *Goodbye to Berlin*, where the boys whistling to their girlfriends from the street below intensifies the narrator's solitude, Isherwood writes: 'In real life, the whistling would only have worried Christopher on some occasion when a boy was whistling for him and he was afraid that Otto, who had a key, might show up unexpectedly and find them together and make a scene' (CK, 59).

Indeed, where *Lions and Shadows* is an autobiography of Isherwood as a writer and his rebellion against the others – the poshocracy, Laily and the dons – *Christopher and His Kind* is an autobiography of himself as a homosexual where the others have morphed into heterosexuals, with Kathleen as their figurehead. For example, after recounting his one-night stand with Mrs Lanigan, Christopher supposedly considers a life of easeful heterosexual conformity, before indignantly banishing the idea:

> Girls are what the state and the church and the law and the press and the medical profession endorse, and command me to desire. My mother endorses them, too. She is silently brutishly willing me to get married and breed grandchildren for her. Her will is the will of Nearly Everybody, and in their will is my death. (CK, 12)

Isherwood's hatred of Kathleen's conformity seems to stem from the original sin of her heterosexuality. In revenge for Kathleen's conventional desire that Richard go to university, 'Christopher told her coldly and aggressively about his life in Berlin. He made his acts of homosexual love sound like acts of defiance, directed against Kathleen' (CK, 39). Kathleen's account of the event in her diary is altogether less dramatic: 'Christopher in to lunch and we talked most of the afternoon, largely on sex.'[14] Isherwood claims that such was her intransigence regarding Richard's upbringing, he called in the anthropologist John Layard to see her. Layard held that sin consisted in repressing one's desires, and, according to Isherwood, he spoke to Kathleen 'with his usual bluntness', and 'she agreed meekly that she had made many mistakes' (*CK*, 39). Again, Kathleen's diary is at variance with her son's mythic version of events: 'Christopher had Mr Layard to tea upstairs and invited R. to meet him. I was out to tea but got back about six and saw Mr Layard for a few minutes.'[15] There scarcely seems time for Kathleen's *mea culpa* regarding Richard, and it was Richard, rather than Kathleen, whom Layard had been invited to meet.

In *Christopher and His Kind*, all the key decisions of Isherwood's life are represented as imbricated with his sexuality. After he quits Berlin, his restless wanderings around Europe are because of his relationship with Heinz. The fuzzy comradely feelings he felt for the communists in Berlin are nullified when he learns that Stalin has outlawed homosexuality:

> He now realized he must dissociate himself from the Communists, even as a fellow traveler . . . He must never again give way to embarrassment, never deny the rights of his tribe, never apologize for its existence, never think of sacrificing himself masochistically on the altar of that false god of the totalitarians, the Greatest Good of the Greatest Number – whose priests are alone empowered to decide what 'good' is. (*CK*, 346)

And his conversion to pacifism is inspired by the following reflection: 'I have a Nazi Army at my mercy. I can blow it up by pressing a button. The men in that Army are notorious for torturing and murdering civilians – all except for one of them, Heinz. Will I press the button?' (*CK*, 347). In his review of the book, Edward Upward emphasized the *literary* component of Isherwood's identity: 'To be a writer was even more essential to him than to be a homosexual. Creativity was the supreme law of his own nature it would be death for him to disobey – though he never explicitly says so in this book.' Furthermore, he argued that Isherwood emigrated to the United States in 1939 because he hoped he 'would become free there to develop along the lines that were natural to him as a writer'.[16]

When *Christopher and His Kind* was published by Farrar, Straus and Giroux in September 1976, it was largely praised by the critics. The reviewer in the *TLS* wrote that Isherwood's 'prose is as impeccable and irresistible as ever', and opined that he was 'the funniest English writer' since Evelyn Waugh.[17] There were, however, a few homophobic naysayers, such as Rebecca West, who asserted that the book was replete with 'male prostitutes' and 'dirty, drunken', disease-ridden men whose 'existence. . . is one long symphony of squalor'.[18] But these barbs were more than compensated for by the reaction of Isherwood's 'kind'. 'Perhaps the most moving experience', he wrote, apropos his promotional tour of New York,

> was going down to the Oscar Wilde Memorial Bookshop in the village and signing copies of my book, with a line of people, mostly quite young, stretching all the way down Christopher Street and around the corner. I had such a feeling that this is my tribe and I loved them. (*D3*, 530)

As he got older, Isherwood spent more and more time with Prabhavananda, who was now over eighty and in declining health. In addition, he stepped up his devotions at Ivar Avenue, participating in some of the *pujas* and regularly giving readings at the temple. Not long after finishing *Christopher and His Kind*, he made a trip to Tangier, where he learned that Prabhavananda had died on 4 July 1976, and flew back to America to attend the memorial service. In the wake of the swami's death, he dismissed the idea of writing the American sequel to *Christopher and His Kind* and decided to write a memoir about Prabhavananda. In fact, the subjective nature of his memoir meant that it was partly 'about Christopher', and so much of the material slated for volume two of *Christopher and His Kind* appeared in *My Guru and His Disciple*.

He wrongly predicted that *My Guru* would be a slim volume like *Prater Violet*. 'Perhaps the best thing about it will be its final passage, a description of me in old age and of what Swami means to me now

Christopher Isherwood, *c.* early 1970s, by Jerry Bauer.

that he is dead' (*D*3, 538–9). He had almost finished a first draft by October 1977, but found himself devoid of inspiration for the last chapter concerning the enduring presence of Prabhavananda and the comfort it afforded him as he contemplated death. The chief problem was that, as he admitted in his diary, 'I have never once really felt Swami's presence since he died' (*D*3, 560). He was also none too sanguine about the slings and arrows of old age. At the start of 1978 he tore a ligament in his knee while jogging. 'The weather is glorious,' he wrote in February, 'and I can't run down to the beach. Maybe I never will again' (*D*3, 564). In addition, he was losing his hair and the sight in his left eye was impaired due to a cataract. As for his mind, his powers of concentration were waning, and he found the revisions of *My Guru* so exhausting that he suspected he might have had a stroke.

The book picks up the narrative from *Christopher and His Kind*, with the arrival in New York of Auden and himself in January 1939. It is largely composed of edited diary entries, with co-ordinating passages to bridge the narrative gaps. Isherwood had long toyed with the idea of publishing his diaries from 1939 to 1944, and the first twelve chapters of *My Guru* partly fulfil this ambition, in that they chart his migration to Los Angeles, his involvement with Gerald Heard, his conversion to Vedanta and his monastic training at Ivar Avenue. The remaining eight chapters are more amorphous in comparison and consist of descriptions of Prabhavananda during Isherwood's householder years, when he made guilty trips to Ivar Avenue and Trabuco for special occasions, such as Vivekananda's birthday *puja*, during which he would read the *Katha Upanishad*.

Isherwood was temperamentally unsuited to the devotional life, and it is a tribute to Prabhavananda that his wayward disciple didn't turn his back on Ivar Avenue after the war. It was Prabhavananda's example, his unwavering faith, the hours and hours of *japam* and meditation, that bolstered Isherwood's faith. '*Watching Swami huddled in his chadar before the shrine . . . I thought: He's been doing this all his life. He isn't kidding*' (*MG*, 255).[19] For his part, Prabhavananda never gave up on Isherwood, and zealously attempted to lead him back to the monastic fold. For example, when Prabhavananda made 'an approving remark about the look in Don's face' on first meeting Bachardy, Isherwood inferred this as his sanction of their relationship. A few years later, though, when Prabhavananda suggested that Bachardy and Isherwood move into a Vedanta property near the temple, Isherwood perceived this as the 'first move in another back-to-the-monastery campaign' (*MG*, 234). Prabhavananda repeatedly urged Isherwood to return to Ivar Avenue, and in 1962 he even offered to make Isherwood a swami, a process that would ordinarily take ten years.

On the one hand, Isherwood's work on the translations of the *Gita* and other Hindu texts, as well as his biography of Ramakrishna, can be interpreted as Prabhavananda keeping his disciple close; on the other hand, Prabhavananda took advantage of Isherwood's

Isherwood at the Father's Day celebration, 19 June 1960, honouring Swami Prabhavananda as his spiritual father.

literary skills and doubtless hoped that his fame would help attract new Vedanta converts. Isherwood reproduces Fouts's assessment of Prabhavananda from his diary:

> *According to him, Swami is bound to accept me on any terms, because I'm so useful to the Vedanta Society as a translator and editor. I get very angry when he talks like this, and I think it's utterly unjust to Swami. But the fact remains that he is much less lenient toward most of the others.* (*MG*, 163–4)

Moreover, in another context (his fraught relationship with John Yale), he remarks: 'My visits to Swami were like those of a Prodigal Son who returns home again and again, without the least intention of staying, and is always uncritically welcomed by a Father who scolds every other member of the family for the smallest backsliding' (*MG*, 216).

What's missing from these householder years is any sense of Isherwood's spiritual frustrations and doubts. These can be found *passim* in his diaries, and yet he purposely omits them from *My Guru*, perhaps feeling that they are not relevant to his portrait of Prabhavananda. For example, this diary entry from April 1966:

> Talking of maya, my spiritual life couldn't possibly be deader. I say my beads every morning in front of the *Life Magazine* photograph of Swami at the shrine. And now I wrap myself in the *chadar* he gave me. Does it help at all? Apparently not, but . . . what's the alternative? (*D2*, 393)

He does, however, readily admit to the proxy nature of his faith in *My Guru*: '*My religion is almost entirely what I glimpse of Swami's spiritual experience*' (*MG*, 308–9). It is perhaps unsurprising, then, that after Prabhavananda's death Isherwood rejects 'Swami's Hindu pantheon of gods, goddesses, and divine incarnations', whereas 'Ramakrishna, Brahmananda, Vivekananda, and Holy Mother remain to inspire me as powerfully individual figures' (*MG*, 335).[20] In other words, it is these human saints rather than abstract

Hindu gods that Isherwood finds inspiring. In the epilogue, as he contemplates the end of life, he maintains that if death doesn't bring annihilation, it will be as Prabhavananda predicted: rebirth for those with karmic debt and liberation for the enlightened. What worries him, though, is the prospect of finding himself in the 'Ramakrisha loka' – a sort of Vedantic heaven – with Ramakrishna, Holy Mother and Prabhavananda as his eternal companions.

Epilogue

My Guru and His Disciple was published in the summer of 1980. It was the last full-length book Isherwood completed in his lifetime. A few years earlier, he had been commissioned to write a commentary for a book of Bachardy's celebrity portraits. But while Bachardy's early work had been boosted by the fame of his sitters, he was now an acclaimed artist in his own right, and the book they finally published comprises Isherwood's diary from October 1979 accompanied by Bachardy's portraits of their friends (most of whom were not famous). Titled *October*, the book was published the following year and opens with a poignant recollection of Isherwood's brother, who had died of a heart attack in May 1978: 'My brother Richard's birthday. Today he would have been sixty-eight years old.'[1] Not long after Kathleen's death, Richard had moved in with some friends, the Bradleys, in the nearby village of Disley. In a letter of condolence, Mrs Bradley reported that in the week preceding his death, Richard had sensed that he was going to die, as he'd been visited by flashbacks of his life. He 'died in the arms of Dan', she wrote, referring to her husband, 'whom he loved'.[2]

Now in his seventies, Isherwood received a pension, and one of the livelier entries from *October* concerns queuing in the bank to deposit his cheque alongside his fellow pensioners. He endeavours to distance himself from them on the grounds that he is less needy and 'decrepit', before confessing that he does not want to join the ranks of the retired. 'I try to persuade myself that I will always be able to function somehow, to some extent, right to the last – and that I will always have a project, even if I know it can never be completed.'³ Isherwood's new project was another autobiography of his life in America. The idea was to write about the more secular aspects of his American career, such as his film work, his famous friends and so forth, by examining them through the lens of the different properties he'd lived in since moving to LA. His house on Adelaide Drive would serve as a metaphor for himself in old age, with its erosion and disrepair. But instead of plunging in headfirst as was his habit, he confined himself to jotting down ideas in his diary, and he didn't make a start on the book until May 1981.

Around this time, he noted that he was losing weight – a bad sign in someone who had given up jogging and no longer went to the gym. He had also lost his appetite and was nauseated by the aroma of food. In September, alarmed by his weight loss and plagued by back pain, he was admitted to hospital, where he was subsequently diagnosed with prostate cancer.[4] 'Well, the moment has come when I must recognize and discuss the situation with myself,' he wrote in his diary.

> I have got some sort of malignancy, a tumor, and that's what's behind all this pain. They will treat it, of course, and so we shall enter the cancer-recognition phase and its gradual retreat to the terminal. I shall get used to the idea, subject to fits of blind panic. The pain may actually be lessened but there will be the constant awareness of it. Before all, there will be the need to accept what is going to happen. My goodness – at my age, should that be so difficult? No, it shouldn't be. Yes, but it will be. (*D*3, 679)

There followed a three-month hiatus in his diary, which he attributed to 'the dreariest, most cowardly depression' (*D*3, 680). But he seems to have been encouraged by his doctor's assurance that the cancer could be held in abeyance by medication, and by February 1982 he reported that he'd completed 94 pages of the book he was now calling *Scenes from an Emigration*. As with *My Guru and His Disciple*, though, most of the manuscript was composed of excerpts from his diaries, and while he never consciously abandoned the book, he slowly came to a halt that summer.

For the next three years, Bachardy affirmed, Isherwood was in 'relatively good health, though he *was* dwindling, mentally as well as physically'.[5] He stopped writing letters and his diary entries grew more and more erratic and finally petered out on 4 July 1983, exactly seven years after Prabhavananda's death. For more than a decade, Isherwood had prayed to Ramakrishna to be with him 'in the hour of death', which seems an oddly Catholic sentiment for a Hindu, echoing the Ave Maria: 'Holy Mary, mother of God, pray for us sinners, now, and in the hour of death. Amen.' The devout Catholic prays to St Mary in the hour of death because she fears she may go to hell for her sins, whereas the worst a devout, or even an ambivalent, Hindu faces is rebirth. Now that Isherwood was dying, he prayed to Prabhavananda, entreating him to be present 'Now and in the hour of death' (*D*3, 681). Sometimes this was consoling, while at others he was filled with doubts and had to rationalize Prabhavananda's 'presence':

> Swami really is present within me because I remember him. Why shouldn't I remember him when I am dying and get strength and reassurance from that memory? In the last analysis, strength and reassurance are all I'm asking for. Looked at from this point of view, my problem doesn't have to be solved by 'faith.' I just have to relive one of those powerful experiences of reassurance which I quite often had in his presence while he was still alive. (*D*3, 686)

It is characteristic that Isherwood prayed to Prabhavananda, rather than a Hindu deity, to supply the faith he lacked.

In the last six months of his life, Isherwood was beset by pain. He and Bachardy still occasionally entertained, and a close friend recalled that Isherwood 'would unexpectedly scream at any point, then act as if nothing had happened', while the distraught guests would pretend to 'ignore the outburst'.[6] During this time, Bachardy gave up his other models and focused exclusively on painting

Isherwood. 'He grimaces with pain as he inches his rump towards the pillows,' Bachardy noted in his diary, 'often letting out piercing cries. "If you *knew* what it's like, this pain!" he often says to me, as though reprimanding me.'[7] While Bachardy often felt guilty for exacerbating his partner's pain during these sessions, which lasted for hours, he asserted: 'it is the only way now that I can really be with him intensely, in a way which challenges me as much as him.'[8] It was at once a coping strategy and a means of participating in his death. Towards the end, Bachardy had to goad himself to continue: 'I have real trouble now just looking at him, torn as I am between sympathy and disgust.'[9] At this point, Isherwood was largely unaware of what was happening, and lay on his bed moaning, maundering, crying for his nanny. Bachardy refused to have him admitted to hospital for a morphine drip, because he knew that his partner wanted to die at home, and because he wanted to draw Isherwood after his death and worried that he'd be prevented from doing so in hospital.

Isherwood died on the morning of 4 January 1986. Before embarking on his post-mortem drawings, Bachardy noted in his diary: 'Chris's body spooks me because already it has so little to do with him. Wherever he is, he is not in *that*.'[10] For the next seven hours, Bachardy made eleven drawings of the body, stopping only because the doctor was due to arrive to certify the death. He included four of these post-mortem portraits in his heroic book *Christopher Isherwood: Last Drawings* (1990). It is a fitting tribute to a writer who fearlessly disclosed the minutiae of his private life in his work that even his dying was documented in this manner. Several of the portraits are nudes and reveal the small breasts Isherwood had developed as a result of being given oestrogen to inhibit the cancer. In the early portraits from the summer of 1985, Isherwood appears reasonably self-possessed, an alert participant in the portrait. But as the autumn and winter come on, his skull becomes more noticeable through the friable skin, and his face betrays, by turns, resignation, misery and abject fear. The last of the living portraits capture Isherwood's bewilderment and agony – his eyes closed, as if to shut in the despair. In the post-mortem drawings, his sightless eyes are open, his mouth ajar revealing his few remaining teeth, and beyond that – a void. 'I was deeply shocked by Chris's remains,' wrote Bachardy afterwards, 'their utter lack of connection with him . . . but forced myself to go on and on, looking into those dead empty eyes where once such light had flashed.'[11]

Isherwood's work on *Scenes from an Emigration* was part of his ongoing ambition to write the *whole* of his life. He spent the first two-thirds of his career writing autobiographical fictions, and the last third writing fictionalized autobiography, as if preparing the reader for the last instalment of the Isherwood oeuvre: his diaries. In July 1980, while still contemplating *Scenes*, he wrote in his diary: 'I still haven't begun work on my next autobiographical book . . . What if I die? Oh well, the diaries are there – let someone else fuss around with them' (*D3*, 639). It is not to be regretted that he never completed *Scenes*, and that someone else, namely Katherine Bucknell, assiduously edited his diaries and published them in three volumes (1996–2012). The published *Diaries* run to more than a million words and can be considered alongside the best of his work. Bachardy observed that Isherwood disparaged the diaries of other writers for being written with one eye on posterity, whereas Isherwood's diaries were composed 'out of an inner need to record his life', and were written spontaneously, without revision.[12]

In his best novels – *Goodbye to Berlin*, *Prater Violet*, *A Single Man* – Isherwood subjected the coal of his experience to a kind of artistic compression that produced a diamond purged of all repetition, digression and banality. In contrast, Isherwood faithfully recorded the quotidian texture of his life in his diaries: going to the gym, swimming in the sea, obsessing about his weight – all the things, in other words, that the novelist leaves out. In *Christopher and His Kind*, Isherwood notes that he received many letters from young fans who lamented that they hadn't lived in Berlin at the same time as Herr Issyvoo: 'This is flattering but also ironic; for most of them could no more have shared Christopher's life in Berlin than they could have lived with a hermit in the desert. Not because of any austerities Christopher endured. Because of the boredom' (*CK*, 193–4).

In his diaries, then, Isherwood recuperated the artful gaps and ellipses of his fiction and presented his life as lived, free from the artificial drama and concision of his fiction that had, among other things, neutered Herr Issyvoo.

One of Herr Issyvoo's charms is his self-effacing absorption in other people, and so it came as a shock to some critics to be confronted with this massive record of the author's life. Moreover, many reviewers judged his diaries by the standards of his fiction and complained that they were boring and repetitive. One critic, after acknowledging that Isherwood was 'his own subject', objected that in his diaries 'there is simply no space for other people'.[13] On the one hand, it should surely come as no surprise that Isherwood wrote about himself in his diaries; on the other, the diaries are full of deft anecdotes and sketches of friends, lovers, writers, actors, artists, politicians, directors and Vedanta devotees, as well as cleaners, handymen, doctors and neighbours. The same critic was also scandalized by Isherwood's use of clichés: 'It is cold in London, and it rains. He likes the weather in California,' and he describes the Alps as 'magnificent'.[14]

Other critics were keen to call out Isherwood for his inveterate antisemitism and misogyny. More than one reviewer indignantly quoted Isherwood's judgement of Dodie Smith's novel *A Tale of Two Families* (1970):

> It's so pleased with itself, so fucking smug, so snugly cunty, the art of women who are delighted with themselves, who indulge themselves and who patronize their men. They *know* that there is nothing, there *can* be nothing outside of the furry rim of their cunts and their kitchens, their children and their clubs. (*D*3, 40–41)[15]

This misogynistic rant was inspired by Isherwood's resentment that, prior to a visit with Smith, he felt obliged to read her new book, and he always rebelled at any kind of obligation. In a more temperate entry he praised Smith for being 'extraordinarily sensitive and intelligent' (*D*1, 259), and he dedicated *The World in the Evening* to Smith and her husband in recognition of their friendship and literary advice.

In 1971 Isherwood had attempted to reconstruct the lost years (1945–53) with Bill Caskey, when he'd all but ceased to keep a diary, piecing it together from appointment books and letters from the period. He described the project as 'quite largely a sexual record and so indiscreet as to be unpublishable' (*D3*, 119). Although he never completed this project (only reaching the year 1951), it was published under the title *Lost Years* in 2000, and was met with widespread condemnation. Even critics who had admired volume one of Isherwood's *Diaries* were dismayed by the book: 'This shows Christopher Isherwood at his worst: solipsistic, trivial, self-obsessed, bitchy, manipulative, immature, self-indulgent, guilt-ridden, filthy-minded, stupid with drink, spiritually flushed and morally bankrupt.'[16] Part of the problem, one suspects, is that the book was 'largely a sexual record', and most critics are loath to praise a book in which the author has more sex than them, although their disapproval must be displaced onto other matters. Several reviewers objected that in this sexual record there was no historical perspective, and quoted Isherwood's own retrospective criticism that on the day Mussolini and his mistress were killed he recorded in his diary that he went to the beach and stayed the night with Denny Fouts.[17] In a similar vein, David Thomson lamented that Isherwood's 'camera' had nothing to say about McCarthyism, the atom bomb and Auschwitz.[18] Peter Ackroyd, one of the few critics who actually liked the book, noted in his review that on the night of the Nazi surrender Isherwood had drinks with Aldous Huxley: 'Another diarist might well have invented suitable sentiments, or recalled that evening's conversation in a roseate glow, but Isherwood does nothing of the kind,' he wrote. 'There, perhaps, lies his honesty.'[19]

If *Lost Years* marked the nadir of Isherwood's posthumous reputation, with many of his books being out of print, the twenty-first century has seen a pronounced uptick of interest in his work. In 1999 Isherwood's papers were acquired by the Huntington Library in San Marino, California, for a reputed seven-figure sum, and this led to a series of new academic publications, such as *Conversations with Christopher Isherwood* (2001), *Kathleen and Christopher: Christopher Isherwood's Letters to His Mother* (2005), *Isherwood on Writing: The Lectures in California* (2007) and *The Animals: Love Letters between Christopher Isherwood and Don Bachardy* (2013). The Huntington has hosted lectures, exhibits and a conference on Isherwood's work, which resulted in a collection of essays.[20] In 2001 the Christopher Isherwood Foundation was established, and its generous grants have enabled many scholars to conduct research in the Isherwood archive at the Huntington. Beyond the academy, Isherwood's work has reached a new audience through the film adaptations of *A Single Man* (2009), directed by Tom Ford, and *Christopher and His Kind* (2011), a BBC film with a script by Kevin Elyot, as well as the release of the documentary *Chris and Don: A Love Story* (2007), which focuses on Isherwood's 33-year relationship with Bachardy. This new wave of popular interest has led to the republication of all Isherwood's work in the UK with Vintage Modern Classics and a large selection in the USA with Farrar, Straus and Giroux.

Isherwood's work inspired subsequent generations of gay writers. Truman Capote's most famous character, Holly Golightly, was a homage to Sally Bowles, and Bucknell claims that the form of Capote's non-fiction novel *In Cold Blood* (1966) was indebted to Isherwood's autofiction.[21] Edmund White named Isherwood as one of his literary mentors,[22] and judged *A Single Man* 'one of the first and best novels of the modern gay liberation movement'.[23] Indeed, the influence of *A Single Man* can be felt on White's novel *The Married Man* (2000), as well as *The Beauty of Men* (1996) by Andrew Holleran.[24] In his memoir, Armistead Maupin wrote that *Goodbye to Berlin* 'had not only set the tone for my life in San Francisco but had also offered a template' for *Tales of the City* (1978), which 'took place in a shabby apartment house with an all-seeing landlady and carnally adventurous tenants'.[25] Maupin conducted Isherwood's last interview for the *Village Voice* in 1985, and recalled his uncompromising advice for the men who were diagnosed with AIDS:

They're told by their relatives that it's a sort of punishment, that it's . . . God's will and all that kind of thing. And I think they have to get very tough with themselves and really decide which side they're on. You know, fuck God's will. God's will must be circumvented, if that's what it is.[26]

Perhaps inevitably, in the mind of the public, Isherwood is still best known for having inspired the musical *Cabaret*. After the success of the film version in 1972, there were several long-running revivals of *Cabaret* in London's West End and on Broadway, for example the acclaimed Sam Mendes production at the Donmar Warehouse in 1993, with Jane Horrocks in the role of Sally Bowles and Alan Cumming as the Emcee. More recently, there has been a West End revival at the Playhouse Theatre in 2021, and on Broadway at the August Wilson Theatre in 2024. In the LGBTQIA community, Isherwood's renown also rests on *A Single Man* and *Christopher and His Kind*. Going forwards, it is to be hoped that his *Diaries* will attract a wider readership. Granted, Isherwood's best fiction is succinct, but the *Diaries* can be read as his epic – his *War and Peace*, or perhaps his *Remembrance of Things Past*. While the individual days might seem unextraordinary – full of pottering, weather and fugitive recrimination – they add up to a monumental life.

References

Introduction: Autofiction

1 See George Orwell, *Inside the Whale and Other Essays* (London, 1940), p. 152.
2 *Mr Norris Changes Trains* was published under the title *The Last of Mr Norris* in America.
3 See James J. Berg and Chris Freeman's essay collections: *The Isherwood Century: Essays on the Life and Work of Christopher Isherwood* (Madison, WI, and London, 2000), *The American Isherwood* (Minneapolis, MN, and London, 2015) and *Isherwood in Transit* (Minneapolis, MN, and London, 2020).
4 See James J. Berg, ed., *Isherwood on Writing: The Lectures in California* (Minneapolis, MN, and London, 2007), p. 166.
5 See, for example, Anne Taylor Fleming, 'Christopher Isherwood: He Is a Camera', in *Conversations with Christopher Isherwood*, ed. James J. Berg and Chris Freeman (Jackson, MS, 2001), pp. 90–97 (p. 94).
6 See Armistead Maupin, foreword to *The Isherwood Century*, ed. Berg and Freeman, p. xiii.
7 See Jaime Harker, *Middlebrow Queer: Christopher Isherwood in America* (Minneapolis, MN, 2013), p. xiv.
8 See, for example, Edmund White, 'Today the Artist Is a Saint Who Writes His Own life', *London Review of Books*, available at www.lrb.co.uk, 9 March 1995, and Eveline Kilian, '"The Mystery-Magic of Foreignness": Mr Isherwood Changes Places', in *Life Writing and Space*, ed. Eveline Kilian and Hope Wolf (Abingdon and New York, 2016), pp. 89–104 (p. 91).
9 Quoted in Claudia Gronemann, 'Autofiction', in *Handbook of Autobiography/Autofiction*, ed. Martina Wagner-Egelhaaf (Berlin and Boston, MA, 2019), pp. 241–6 (p. 241).

10 See ibid. and Karen Ferreira-Meyers, 'Does Autofiction Belong to French or Francophone Authors and Readers Only?', in *Autofiction in English*, ed. Hywel Dix (London, 2018), pp. 27–48 (p. 28).
11 Dix, introduction to *Autofiction in English*, p. 7.
12 See Claire Battershill, 'Reticent Autobiography: Henry Green and Christopher Isherwood at the Hogarth Press', *Journal of Modern Literature*, XXXIX/1 (2015), pp. 38–54 (p. 39).
13 See Stephen Spender, 'Notebook – XII', *London Magazine*, 1 April 1977, p. 50.
14 Smith quoted in Peter Parker, *Isherwood: A Life* (London, 2004), p. 554.
15 The annoying exception is *A Single Man*, which, despite being highly autobiographical, features a protagonist named George and is narrated in the third person.
16 White, 'Today the Artist Is a Saint Who Writes His Own Life'.
17 Ibid.

1 The Poshocracy, 1904–25

1 Isherwood notes that his early ancestors spelt Bradshaw with a terminal 'e'. See *KF*, p. 295.
2 In both *Kathleen and Frank* and *Christopher and His Kind*, Isherwood refers to his younger self as 'Christopher' in order to hone his objectivity.
3 Christopher Isherwood, *Exhumations: Stories, Articles, Verses* (London, 1966), p. 170.
4 Latin adage from Horace: 'It is sweet and fitting to die for the fatherland.'
5 See Kathleen Isherwood, 'The Baby's Progress', in CIP (CI 591).
6 Katherine Bucknell, *Christopher Isherwood Inside Out* (New York, 2024), p. 116.
7 Edward Upward, *No Home but the Struggle* (London, 1977), p. 140.
8 Edward Upward, letter to Christopher Isherwood, 31 December 1922, in CIP (CI 2292).
9 See Peter Parker, *Isherwood: A Life* (London, 2004), p. 91.
10 Isherwood borrowed the title from a story collection by C. E. Montague, who floridly refers to his characters as 'arrant lovers of living, mighty hunters of lions or shadows, rapt amateurs of shady adventure or profitless zeal'. See C. E. Montague, *Fiery Particles* (London, 1923), p. vii.

11 See Katherine Bucknell, introduction to Christopher Isherwood and Edward Upward, *The Mortmere Stories*, ed. Katherine Bucknell (London, 1994), p. 13.
12 Christopher Isherwood, foreword to Edward Upward, *The Railway Accident and Other Stories* (Harmondsworth, 1971), p. 33.
13 See Brian Finney, 'Laily, Mortmere and All That', *Twentieth Century Literature*, xxii/3 (1976), pp. 286–302 (p. 293).
14 Isherwood and Upward, *The Mortmere Stories*, p. 63.

2 Tea-Tabling, 1925–30

1 Quoted in Peter Parker, *Isherwood: A Life* (London, 2004), p. 125.
2 See James J. Berg, ed., *Isherwood on Writing: The Lectures in California* (Minneapolis, mn, and London, 2007), p. 56.
3 At any rate, this was how Isherwood portrayed their literary relationship in *Lions and Shadows*. In reality, Auden was more assertive. See Katherine Bucknell, *Christopher Isherwood Inside Out* (New York, 2024), p. 185.
4 There is a section in *Textbook of Psychiatry* titled 'The Aberrations of the Sexual Impulse', in which Bleuler discusses homosexuality. Unlike Freud, who regarded homosexuality as a developmental disorder, Bleuler maintains that homosexuality is congenital and rejects the idea of its being a disease. See Eugen Bleuler, *Textbook of Psychiatry* [1924], trans. A. A. Brill (New York, 1934), pp. 572–82.
5 See Peter Stansky, *Edward Upward: Art and Life* (London, 2016), p. 83.
6 Despite Isherwood's portrait of Weston in *Lions and Shadows* as a natural man in harmony with his libido, Auden's interest in psychoanalysis was also connected to his homosexuality. See Richard R. Bozorth, 'Auden: Love, Sexuality, Desire', in *The Cambridge Companion to W. H. Auden*, ed. Stan Smith (Cambridge, 2005), pp. 179–80.
7 Bleuler, *Textbook of Psychiatry*, p. 531.
8 This figure derives from the Bank of England Inflation Calculator.
9 See Parker, *Isherwood*, pp. 141–2.
10 See Bucknell, *Christopher Isherwood*, p. 189.
11 See *ls*, p. 194.
12 See Brian Finney, *Christopher Isherwood: A Critical Biography* (London, 1979), p. 71.
13 See Lisa M. Schwerdt, *Isherwood's Fiction: The Self and Technique* (Basingstoke and London, 1989), p. 29.

14 See Edward Upward, letter to Christopher Isherwood, n.d., in CIP (CI 2297).
15 Christopher Isherwood, 'Foreword to *All the Conspirators*', in *Exhumations: Stories, Articles, Verses* (London, 1966), p. 92.
16 See Alan Wilde, *Christopher Isherwood* (New York, 1971), p. 33.
17 Berg, ed., *Isherwood on Writing*, p. 150.
18 See Bucknell, *Christopher Isherwood*, p. 193.
19 See Isherwood, *Exhumations*, pp. 91, 124.
20 Quoted in *LS*, p. 206.
21 Quoted in Parker, *Isherwood*, p. 139.
22 Stephen Spender, *World within World* (London, 1951), p. 102. Spender uses the pseudonym Chalmers for Upward, as Isherwood had done in *All the Conspirators* and *Lions and Shadows*.
23 See Edward Mendelson, *Early Auden, Later Auden: A Critical Biography* (Princeton, NJ, and Oxford, 2017), p. 60.
24 See ibid.
25 See Parker, *Isherwood*, pp. 133, 171.
26 See ibid., pp. 177–8.
27 This account from *Christopher and His Kind* is at variance with Auden's journal, in which Isherwood visited the museum with Auden on his first trip to Berlin in March. See Bucknell, *Christopher Isherwood*, p. 205.
28 Quoted in *CK*, p. 18.
29 Edward Upward letter to Isherwood, n.d. [1931], in CIP (CI 2424).
30 Spender, *World within World*, p. 126.
31 Ibid., p. 121.
32 See Mendelson, *Early Auden, Later Auden*, p. 61n.
33 See Finney, *Christopher Isherwood*, p. 98.
34 See Schwerdt, *Isherwood's Fiction*, p. 47.
35 See Wilde, *Christopher Isherwood*, p. 48.

3 The Lost, 1931–7

1 Edward Upward, letter to Isherwood, n.d. [1931], in CIP (CI 2436).
2 See *CK*, p. 61.
3 See Peter Parker, *Isherwood: A Life* (London, 2004), pp. 205–7.
4 See *CK*, p. 62.
5 Donald Windham, ed., *Tennessee Williams' Letters to Donald Windham, 1940–1965* (Harmondsworth and New York, 1980), pp. 89, 94.

6 See Paul Bowles, *Without Stopping* (New York, 1972), pp. 112, 116.
7 Phil Baker, 'Hamilton, Gerald Francis Bernard (1890–1970)', *Oxford Dictionary of National Biography*, www.oxforddnb.com, 3 October 2013.
8 Isherwood was 5 feet 8 inches tall (173 cm).
9 Anon., 'Portrait of a Family', *Times Literary Supplement*, 14 April 1932, p. 272.
10 See Peter Stansky, *Edward Upward: Art and Life* (London, 2016), pp. 132, 137–8.
11 See Stephen Spender, *World within World* (London, 1951), p. 174.
12 Christopher Isherwood, letter to Stephen Spender, 14 November 1932, in CIP (box 122).
13 Christopher Isherwood, letter to Stephen Spender, 3 November 1932, in CIP (box 122).
14 See Christopher Isherwood, unpublished 'Diary of Summer in Greece', in CIP (CI 2749).
15 Ibid.
16 See Parker, *Isherwood*, p. 271.
17 See James J. Berg, ed., *Isherwood on Writing: The Lectures in California* (Minneapolis, MN, and London, 2007), pp. 164–5.
18 See ibid., pp. 57, 165 and CK, p. 192.
19 See Winston Leyland, 'Christopher Isherwood Interview', in *Conversations with Christopher Isherwood*, ed. James J. Berg and Chris Freeman (Jackson, MS, 2001), pp. 98–109 (pp. 100–101).
20 Gerald Hamilton had written a racy novel about an affair between an Englishman and a young Algerian titled *Desert Dreamers* (1914).
21 See Brian Finney, *Christopher Isherwood: A Critical Biography* (London, 1979), pp. 113–14.
22 See Claude J. Summers, *Christopher Isherwood* (New York, 1980), pp. 21–2.
23 Christopher Isherwood, '*Mr Norris and I* by Gerald Hamilton', in *Exhumations: Stories, Articles, Verses* (London, 1966), pp. 86–7.
24 Summers, *Christopher Isherwood*, p. 28.
25 Ibid.
26 William Plomer, *The Spectator*, 1 March 1935, p. 346.
27 Lisa Colletta, ed., *Kathleen and Christopher: Christopher Isherwood's Letters to His Mother* (Minneapolis, MN, and London, 2005), p. 11.
28 Ibid., p. 78.
29 Quoted in Edward Mendelson, *Early Auden, Later Auden: A Critical Biography* (Princeton, NJ, and Oxford, 2017), p. 183.
30 Christopher Isherwood, letter to Stephen Spender, 23 December 1936, in CIP (box 122).

31. See Mendelson, *Early Auden, Later Auden*, p. 183.
32. Christopher Isherwood, unpublished diary 1935–8, 26 May 1937, in CIP (CI 2751).
33. See Parker, *Isherwood*, p. 333.
34. He chose a pseudonym as he didn't want to tarnish his reputation as the communist author of *Journey to a Border* (1938).
35. See his first untitled novel, begun at Repton, in CIP (CI 1143) and the unpublished novel 'Lions and Shadows'.
36. Christopher Isherwood, letter to Stephen Spender, 15 November 1936, in CIP (box 122).
37. James Joyce, *A Portrait of the Artist as a Young Man* [1916] (New York, London and Toronto, 1991), p. 318.
38. Meaning 'shy-making'.
39. Colin Wilson, 'An Integrity Born of Hope: Notes on Christopher Isherwood', *Twentieth Century Literature*, XXII/3 (1976), pp. 312–31 (p. 317). For evil mother readings of Mrs Lindsay, see Finney, *Christopher Isherwood*, p. 73 and Summers, *Christopher Isherwood*, p. 48.

4 Ivar Avenue, 1938–44

1. W. H. Auden and Christopher Isherwood, *Journey to a War* (London, 1939), p. 71.
2. Ibid., pp. 104, 113.
3. As far as I can tell, this is what Isherwood refers to as 'Han Chwang'. In *Journey to a War*, Isherwood and Auden use the now outdated Wade-Giles system to Romanize Chinese place names, whereas I have used the modern Pinyin system (for example, Beijing rather than Peking).
4. Auden and Isherwood, *Journey to a War*, p. 114.
5. Ibid., p. 224.
6. Christopher Isherwood, unpublished diary 1935–8, 20 August 1938, in CIP (CI 2751).
7. See Peter Parker, *Isherwood: A Life* (London, 2004), p. 383.
8. Isherwood gave him the *nom de guerre* Vernon Old in *Christopher and His Kind* and *My Guru and His Disciple*.
9. Christopher Isherwood, unpublished diary 1935–8, 20 August 1938, in CIP (CI 2751).
10. See CK, p. 326.
11. Quoted in John Lehmann, *Isherwood: A Personal Memoir* (New York, 1987), p. 48.

12 See Parker, *Isherwood*, p. 407.
13 See Edward Mendelson, *Early Auden, Later Auden: A Critical Biography* (Princeton, NJ, and Oxford, 2017), p. 309.
14 See Parker, *Isherwood*, p. 418.
15 Lisa Colletta, ed., *Kathleen and Christopher: Christopher Isherwood's Letters to His Mother* (Minneapolis, MN, and London, 2005), p. 127.
16 Ibid., p. 130.
17 See ibid., p. 125.
18 Salinger claimed he had no knowledge of the private detective Hamilton had engaged and that he had defrauded Singer of the money by charging him indefensible legal fees. See Xenobe Purvis, 'A Weakness for Toads', *Times Literary Supplement*, 4 March 2022, pp. 4–5.
19 Colletta, ed., *Kathleen and Christopher*, p. 143.
20 Ibid., p. 131.
21 *Sturmabteilung*, meaning 'Assault Division'.
22 James J. Berg, ed., *Isherwood on Writing: The Lectures in California* (Minneapolis, MN, and London, 2007), p. 166.
23 Claude J. Summers, *Christopher Isherwood* (New York, 1980), p. 32.
24 See Alison Falby, *Between the Pigeonholes: Gerald Heard, 1889–1971* (Newcastle-upon-Tyne, 2008), pp. 12–13; and D1, p. 22.
25 In a monistic system, there is only one category, rather than two. In Advaita Vedanta, that category is *brahman*, and therefore everything is spiritual. Marxism is also a monistic system, and that category is material; so for Marxists, everything is material (there is no soul, no God, no ghosts and so on). Whereas in a dualistic system, there are two categories, for example, mind and body, spiritual and material, metaphysical and physical.
26 The concept of *maya* is frequently misunderstood. It's usually defined as 'illusion', but this does not mean that the phenomenal world is an illusion (like the world in *The Matrix*), for otherwise it would not matter what we did in this hallucinatory world, which would make a mockery of karma. The 'illusion' of *maya* is that we perceive the world as made up of isolated, material things (rocks, rivers, people, peanut butter), when in fact everything is homogeneously spiritual – in other words, *brahman*.
27 Quoted in Parker, *Isherwood*, p. 457.
28 Cyril Connolly, 'Comment', *Horizon*, 1/2 (1940), p. 69.
29 Harold Nicolson, 'People and Things', *The Spectator*, 19 April 1940, p. 555.
30 Quoted in Parker, *Isherwood*, p. 460.

31 Edward Upward, letter to Isherwood, 23 July 1939, in CIP (CI 2455).
32 Christopher Isherwood, letter to Edward Upward, 6 August 1939, in CIP (box 122).
33 This figure derives from the U.S. Inflation Calculator.
34 See introduction to *Vedanta for the Western World*, ed. Christopher Isherwood (London, 1949), pp. 17–26. This is Isherwood's emic version of Ramakrishna's universalism; for a more granular analysis see Jake Poller, *Aldous Huxley and Alternative Spirituality* (Boston, MA, and Leiden, 2019), pp. 105–8.
35 Isherwood, introduction to *Vedanta for the Western World*, p. 1.
36 Quoted in Aldous Huxley, *The Perennial Philosophy* [1945] (New York, 2004), p. 12.
37 Quoted in W. T. Stace, *Mysticism and Philosophy* (London, 1961), p. 88.
38 See Falby, *Between the Pigeonholes*, pp. 14, 106.
39 See Parker, *Isherwood*, p. 454.
40 'Trabuco Prospectus', in the 2009 Aldous Huxley Collection of the Charles E. Young Research Library, UCLA.
41 Ibid.
42 Miriam King, 'Life at Trabuco', www.geraldheard.com, accessed 21 October 2022.
43 *The Song of God: Bhagavad-Gita*, trans. Swami Prabhavananda and Christopher Isherwood [1944] (New York, 1958), p. 37.
44 Ibid., p. 41.
45 See *LY*, p. 5n.

5 *Samsara*, 1945–53

1 Ritual worship, usually including offerings of flowers, food and incense. The Sanskrit word *samsara*, the title of this chapter, denotes both the cycle of rebirth, and the world of impermanence and suffering in which these repeated rebirths take place.
2 See *LY*, p. 49.
3 Quoted in Peter Parker, *Isherwood: A Life* (London, 2004), p. 542.
4 See James J. Berg, ed., *Isherwood on Writing: The Lectures in California* (Minneapolis, MN, and London, 2007), p. 191.
5 Christopher Isherwood, *Exhumations: Stories, Articles, Verses* (London, 1966), p. 143.
6 Christopher Isherwood, *The Condor and the Cows: A South American Travel Diary* [1949] (London, 2013), p. 30.

7 Christopher Isherwood, letter to John Lehmann, 6 November 1948, in CIP (box 121).
8 See Gore Vidal, *Palimpsest: A Memoir* (New York, 1995), p. 187.
9 Christopher Isherwood, 'Writing Notebook', in CIP (CI 1158).
10 William Forthman, 'Memories of Gerald Heard', www.geraldheard.com, accessed 17 April 2018.
11 For a brief period, prior to his living at Ivar Avenue, Isherwood did practise postural or *hatha yoga*, but gave it up when Prabhavananda expressed his disapproval.
12 *How to Know God: The Yoga Aphorisms of Patanjali*, trans. Swami Prabhavananda and Christopher Isherwood [1953] (New York and London, 1969), p. 11.
13 Ibid., p. 16.
14 See Don Bachardy's account of this in the documentary *Chris and Don: A Love Story* (dir. Guido Santi and Tina Mascara, 2007).
15 See Berg, ed., *Isherwood on Writing*, p. 206.
16 Quoted in Brian Finney, *Christopher Isherwood: A Critical Biography* (London, 1979), p. 221.
17 See Parker, *Isherwood*, p. 594.
18 Nonetheless, he maintained that Frank Taylor (a producer at MGM) served as the 'partial model' for Monk while Spender was the 'partial model' for the bisexual Patrick in *A Meeting by the River* (*LY*, pp. 169–70).
19 Berg, ed., *Isherwood on Writing*, p. 210.
20 John Donne, *The Complete English Poems*, ed. A. J. Smith (London, 1996), p. 177.
21 Finney, *Christopher Isherwood*, p. 221.
22 Ibid., p. 222.

6 Kitty and Dobbin, 1954–64

1 See Katherine Bucknell, ed., *The Animals: Love Letters between Christopher Isherwood and Don Bachardy* (London, 2013), pp. ix–x.
2 Christopher Isherwood, 'The Autobiography of My Books', in CIP (CI 1018).
3 Bucknell, ed., *The Animals*, p. 6.
4 See 'The Object of My Nostalgia: Designating the Isherwood-Bachardy Residence and Studio in Los Angeles', www.huntington.org, 21 April 2021.

5. See Amiya's letters to Isherwood from June 1960 in CIP (CI 129–132). The 'pep pills' were possibly 'a powerful and addictive patent sedative' that Richard had been prescribed in the wake of a nervous breakdown during the war. See Katherine Bucknell, *Christopher Isherwood Inside Out* (New York, 2024), p. 391.
6. See Richard Isherwood, letter to Christopher Isherwood, 30 July 1960, in CIP (CI 1369).
7. Bucknell, ed., *The Animals*, p. 49.
8. See ibid., p. 39.
9. Stanley Poss, 'A Conversation on Tape', in *Conversations with Christopher Isherwood*, ed. James J. Berg and Chris Freeman (Jackson, MS, 2001), p. 10.
10. See ibid.
11. Bucknell, *Christopher Isherwood*, p. 562.
12. See Paul Piazza, *Christopher Isherwood: Myth and Anti-Myth* (New York, 1978), pp. 131–2.
13. See Christopher Isherwood, unpublished diary 1935–8, in CIP (CI 2751).
14. In Isherwood's actual diaries from the period, Olive Mangeot, who became a communist in the early 1930s, occupies an analogous position to Mary. For example, Olive complains, like Mary, that all her lodgers will enlist or evacuate to the country.
15. In his unpublished diary, Isherwood recorded the same conversations with Katz as his namesake narrator has with Dr Fisch, for example about the chances of war shifting from fifty–fifty to thirty–seventy.
16. Harris Dienstfrey, 'Personal, Secret Journey', *Commentary*, 1 October 1962, p. 363.
17. Quoted in Peter Parker, *Isherwood: A Life* (London, 2004), p. 695.
18. *Mrs Dalloway* appears on a reading list of books he hadn't 'read right through' in his diary entry for 30 August 1962. See *D2*, p. 184.
19. Literally, 'under the form of eternity'. In other words, viewed from an eternal, impersonal, universal perspective.
20. Henry Kraft is the *nom de guerre* Katherine Bucknell uses to preserve the man's privacy in *D2*. His real name was George Kramer.
21. Christopher Isherwood, 'Girish Ghosh', in CIP (CI 4201).
22. Spender described himself as 'at least a quarter Jewish' in *World within World* (London, 1951), p. 13.
23. Isherwood was clearly aware of this doctrine. See, for instance, Christopher Isherwood, *Ramakrishna and His Disciples* (Hollywood, 1965), p. 62.
24. *The Upanishads*, trans. Juan Mascaró (London, 1965), p. 83.

25 See Arvind Sharma, *A Guide to Hindu Spirituality* (Bloomington, IN, 2006), pp. 82–3.
26 *Upanishads*, p. 83.
27 See Daniel Curley, 'The Reality of Love', *New Leader*, 18 January 1965, p. 23.
28 Claude J. Summers, *Christopher Isherwood* (New York, 1980), p. 117.
29 See Piazza, *Christopher Isherwood*, p. 150.
30 John Gross, 'Civil Monsters', *New Statesman*, 11 September 1964, p. 361.
31 Richard G. Hubler, quoted in Parker, *Isherwood*, p. 726.

7 Life Writing, 1965–80

1 In *Kathleen and Frank*, Isherwood recalls taking an 'erotic' pleasure in watching his father exercising in his underpants when he was a boy (see pp. 354–5).
2 See *D2*, p. 360.
3 Christopher Isherwood, 'The Autobiography of My Books', in CIP (CI 1018).
4 David J. Geherin, 'An Interview with Christopher Isherwood', in *Conversations with Christopher Isherwood*, ed. James J. Berg and Chris Freeman (Jackson, MS, 2001), pp. 74–89 (p. 82).
5 See, for example, John Gross, 'A Question of Upbringing', *New York Review of Books*, 18 May 1967, p. 36.
6 Anon., 'Naked, Not Unashamed', *Times Literary Supplement*, 15 June 1967, p. 525.
7 See Katherine Bucknell, ed., *The Animals: Love Letters between Christopher Isherwood and Don Bachardy* (London, 2013), p. xxiii.
8 See ibid., p. 356.
9 Christopher Isherwood, 'Writing as a Way of Life', 10 February 1965, in CIP (CI 1187).
10 Brian Finney, *Christopher Isherwood: A Critical Biography* (London, 1979), p. 275.
11 See *KF*, p. 240.
12 W. I. Scobie, 'The Youth That Was "I": A Conversation in Santa Monica with Christopher Isherwood', in *Conversations with Christopher Isherwood*, ed. Berg and Freeman, pp. 181–8 (pp. 181–2).
13 Isherwood, 'The Autobiography of My Books'.
14 Excerpt from Kathleen Isherwood's diary, 1 April 1930, in CIP (CI 1411).
15 Excerpt from Kathleen Isherwood's diary, 27 April 1930, ibid.

16 Edward Upward, 'The Resolute Anti-Hero', *New Statesman*, 1 April 1977, p. 434.
17 Gabriele Annan, 'The Issyvoo Years', *Times Literary Supplement*, 1 April 1977, p. 402.
18 Rebecca West, 'A Symphony of Squalor', *Sunday Telegraph*, 3 April 1977, p. 15.
19 In *My Guru*, Isherwood italicizes his diary entries.
20 Holy Mother was the wife of Ramakrishna, whom he married to please his mother; his bride was only five years old at the time and since Ramakrishna became a *sanyasi* or ascetic a few years later, the marriage was never consummated.

Epilogue

1 Christopher Isherwood and Don Bachardy, *October* [1980] (London, 1983), p. 7.
2 Ibid.
3 Ibid., p. 15.
4 See Katherine Bucknell, *Christopher Isherwood Inside Out* (New York, 2024), p. 727.
5 Don Bachardy, *Christopher Isherwood: Last Drawings* (London and Boston, MA, 1990), p. 120.
6 James P. White, 'Write It Down or It's Lost: Isherwood as Mentor', in *The Isherwood Century: Essays on the Life and Work of Christopher Isherwood*, ed. James J. Berg and Chris Freeman (Madison, WI, and London, 2000), pp. 77–86 (p. 85).
7 Bachardy, *Christopher Isherwood*, p. xii.
8 Ibid., p. xv.
9 Ibid., p. xvii.
10 Ibid.
11 Ibid.
12 Niladri R. Chatterjee, 'Portrait of the Artist as Companion: Interviews with Don Bachardy', in *The Isherwood Century*, ed. Berg and Freeman, pp. 97–107 (p. 98). The exception to this rule were the diaries from 1939 to 1944, which Isherwood revised because he allowed other people to read them and often contemplated having them published in his lifetime.
13 Daniel Swift, 'He Was a Camera', *New York Times*, www.nytimes.com, 1 February 2013.

14 Ibid.
15 See, for example, Christopher Bray, 'Excess Baggage – The Voluminous Diaries of Christopher Isherwood', *New Republic*, https://newrepublic.com, 11 January 2013.
16 Ian Sansom, 'Blue Remembered Thrills', *The Guardian*, www.theguardian.com, 1 July 2000.
17 See ibid.
18 David Thomson, 'Out of Film', *New York Times*, www.nytimes.com, 17 September 2000.
19 Peter Ackroyd, 'Go West, Old Man', *The Times*, 21 June 2000, p. 17.
20 Berg and Freeman, eds, *Isherwood in Transit* (Minneapolis, MN, and London, 2020).
21 See Bucknell, *Christopher Isherwood*, p. 398.
22 See Edmund White, preface to *D3*, p. xi.
23 Edmund White, 'Pool in Rocks by the Sea: Isherwood and Bachardy', in *The Isherwood Century*, ed. Berg and Freeman, pp. 121–8 (p. 123).
24 See James J. Berg, ed., introduction to *Isherwood on Writing: The Lectures in California* (Minneapolis, MN, and London, 2007), p. 27.
25 Armistead Maupin, *Logical Family: A Memoir* (London, 2017), p. 254.
26 Quoted in Armistead Maupin, foreword to *The Isherwood Century*, ed. Berg and Freeman, pp. xiii–xiv.

Select Bibliography

Works by Isherwood

All the Conspirators (1928)
The Memorial (1932)
Mr Norris Changes Trains (1935)
The Dog Beneath the Skin with W. H. Auden (1935)
The Ascent of F6 with W. H. Auden (1936)
Sally Bowles (1937)
Lions and Shadows: An Education in the Twenties (1938)
On the Frontier with W. H. Auden (1938)
Goodbye to Berlin (1939)
Journey to a War with W. H. Auden (1939)
Prater Violet (1945)
The Condor and the Cows: A South American Travel Diary (1949)
The World in the Evening (1954)
Down There on a Visit (1962)
A Single Man (1964)
Ramakrishna and His Disciples (1965)
Exhumations: Stories, Articles, Verses (1966)
A Meeting by the River (1967)
Kathleen and Frank (1971)
Frankenstein: The True Story with Don Bachardy (1973)
Christopher and His Kind (1976)
My Guru and His Disciple (1980)
October with Don Bachardy (1980)
People One Ought to Know with Sylvain Mangeot (1982)

Translations

The Intimate Journals of Charles Baudelaire (1930)
The Song of God: Bhagavad-Gita with Swami Prabhavananda (1944)
Shankara's Crest-Jewel of Discrimination with Swami Prabhavananda (1947)
How to Know God: The Yoga Aphorisms of Patanjali with Swami Prabhavananda (1953)

Editor

Vedanta for the Western World (1945)
Vedanta for Modern Man (1952)
Great English Short Stories (1957)

Posthumous Works

Jacob's Hands with Aldous Huxley (1998)
Adjemian, Robert, ed., *The Wishing Tree* (San Francisco, CA, 1987)
Bachardy, Don, and James P. White, eds, *Where Joy Resides: An Isherwood Reader* (London, 1989)
Berg, James J., ed., *Isherwood on Writing: The Lectures in California* (Minneapolis, MN, and London, 2007)
—, and Chris Freeman, eds, *Conversations with Christopher Isherwood* (Jackson, MS, 2001)
Bucknell, Katherine, ed., *The Mortmere Stories* with Edward Upward (London, 1994)
—, *Diaries*, vol. I: *1939–1960* (London, 1996)
—, *Lost Years: A Memoir, 1945–1951* (New York, 2000)
—, *The Sixties: Diaries*, vol. II: *1960–1969* (London, 2010)
—, *Liberation: Diaries*, vol. III: *1970–1983* (New York, 2012)
—, *The Animals: Love Letters between Christopher Isherwood and Don Bachardy* (London, 2013)
Colletta, Lisa, ed., *Kathleen and Christopher: Christopher Isherwood's Letters to His Mother* (Minneapolis, MN, and London, 2005)
Ramsden, George, *The Repton Letters* (Settrington, 1997)
Zeikowitz, Richard E., ed., *Letters between Forster and Isherwood on Homosexuality and Literature* (Basingstoke and New York, 2008)

Works on Isherwood

Berg, James J., and Chris Freeman, eds, *The Isherwood Century: Essays on the Life and Work of Christopher Isherwood* (Madison, WI, and London, 2000)
—, *The American Isherwood* (Minneapolis, MN, and London, 2015)
—, *Isherwood in Transit* (Minneapolis, MN, and London, 2020)
Bucknell, Katherine, *Christopher Isherwood Inside Out* (New York, 2024)
Finney, Brian, 'Laily, Mortmere and All That', *Twentieth Century Literature*, XXII/3 (1976), pp. 286–302
—, *Christopher Isherwood: A Critical Biography* (London, 1979)
Fryer, Jonathan, *Isherwood: A Biography of Christopher Isherwood* (London, 1977)
Harker, Jaime, *Middlebrow Queer: Christopher Isherwood in America* (Minneapolis, MN, and London, 2013)
Izzo, David Garrett, *Christopher Isherwood: His Era, His Gang, and the Legacy of the Truly Strong Man* (Columbia, SC, 2001)
Kamel, Rose, '"Unravelling One's Personal Myth": Christopher Isherwood's Autobiographical Strategies', *Biography*, V/2 (1982), pp. 161–75
Lehmann, John, *Isherwood: A Personal Memoir* (New York, 1987)
Marsh, Victor, 'Advaita Vedanta and the Repositioning of Subjectivity in the Life-Writing of Christopher Isherwood, "Homosexualist"', *Theology and Sexuality*, XV/1 (2009), pp. 97–120
—, 'On "The Problem of the Religious Novel": Christopher Isherwood and "A Single Man"', *Literature and Theology*, XXIV/4 (2010), pp. 378–96
Monnickendam, Andrew, 'Goodbye to Isherwood: The Rise and Fall of a Literary Reputation', *Atlantis: Journal of the Spanish Association of Anglo-American Studies*, XXX/2 (2008), pp. 125–37
Nagarajan, S., 'Christopher Isherwood and the Vedantic Novel: A Study of "A Single Man"', *Ariel – A Review of International English Literature*, III/4 (1972), pp. 63–71
Parker, Peter, *Isherwood: A Life* (London, 2004)
Piazza, Paul, *Christopher Isherwood: Myth and Anti-Myth* (New York, 1978)
Purvis, Xenobe, 'A Weakness for Toads', *Times Literary Supplement*, 4 March 2022, pp. 3–5
Schwerdt, Lisa M., *Isherwood's Fiction: The Self and Technique* (Houndmills and London, 1989)
Summers, Claude J., *Christopher Isherwood* (New York, 1980)

Wilde, Alan, 'Irony and Style: The Example of Christopher Isherwood', *Modern Fiction Studies*, XVI/4 (1970–71), pp. 475–89
——, *Christopher Isherwood* (New York, 1971)
——, 'Language and Surface: Isherwood and the Thirties', *Contemporary Literature*, XVI/4 (1975), pp. 478–91
Wilson, Colin, 'An Integrity Born of Hope: Notes on Christopher Isherwood', *Twentieth Century Literature*, XXII/3 (1976), pp. 312–31

Acknowledgements

First, I would like to thank the team at Reaktion: Vivian Constantinopoulos, Alex Ciobanu and Amy Salter – it's been a pleasure working with you all again. I'm grateful to the Christopher Isherwood Foundation and the Huntington Library for awarding me the Christopher Isherwood Fellowship for 2023–4, which enabled me to spend a month researching the Isherwood archive at the Huntington. Special thanks to James Penner, whose company kept me from going stir crazy in the archive, and who generously agreed to drive me to Trabuco. Thanks to Jon and Anna Monday, who kindly gave James and I the guided tour of Trabuco and introduced us to Swami Dhyanayogananda, who patiently answered all my Vedanta questions. That day at Trabuco was one of the highlights of my trip to Los Angeles. Jon and Anna also provided me with some of the photos in this book, and put me in touch with Swami Vedamritananda, who granted me permission to use the photos of Trabuco and the Hollywood Vedanta Center. A big thank you to Dana Sawyer, who introduced me to Jon and Anna, and who gave me some valuable notes on the Vedanta sections of my book.

I'd like to thank Katherine Bucknell, who provided me with a proof copy of her biography of Isherwood and helped me with the provenance of certain photos. Peter Parker also helped me with photo enquiries, for which I'm grateful. Many thanks to Logan Esdale at the Van Vechten Trust, who waived the fee for the photo of Auden and Isherwood. I'm also grateful to Kathy Allinson for permission to quote from Edward Upward's unpublished letters in the Huntington archive.

A final thank you to Luke Ingram at the Wylie Agency, who arranged the photo and quotation permissions with the Isherwood Estate. Quotations from Isherwood's unpublished work are © 2025, Don Bachardy, used by permission of The Wylie Agency (UK) Limited.

Photo Acknowledgements

The author and publishers wish to express their thanks to the sources listed below for illustrative material and/or permission to reproduce it. Every effort has been made to contact copyright holders; should there be any we have been unable to reach or to whom inaccurate acknowledgements have been made please contact the publishers, and full adjustments will be made to any subsequent printings.

Alamy Stock Photo: pp. 73 (Archivio GBB), 117 (Asphalt Stars Productions/Album), 153 (© Zeitgeist Films/Everett Collection Inc); © 2025 Don Bachardy, used by permission of The Wylie Agency (UK) Limited: pp. 23 (photo The Huntington Library, Art Museum and Botanical Gardens, San Marino, CA), 52, 55, 111; Bridgeman Images: p. 8; Estate of Dodie Smith: p. 103; photos Jake Poller: pp. 92, 115; © Van Vechten Trust, photo Carl Van Vechten Papers, Beinecke Rare Book and Manuscript Library, Yale University, New Haven, CT (YCAL MSS 1050): p. 160; © Vedanta Society of Southern California, used with permission: pp. 84, 86, 93, 114, 139, 166.

'This is the Christopher Isherwood biography we have been missing: informative, readable, and concise. Jake Poller covers both Isherwood's "monumental life" and his considerable work without producing a doorstop . . . he provides fresh insight without being dogmatic, offering alternate readings of events and works. This is a book Isherwood fans will learn from and enjoy.'
– James J. Berg, editor of *Isherwood on Writing*

The year 1939 was pivotal for Christopher Isherwood: he emigrated to the United States and his novel *Goodbye to Berlin*, which inspired the hit musical *Cabaret*, was feted by critics for its portrait of a city under the shadow of fascism. During the Second World War, Isherwood became a pacifist and studied in a Hindu monastery, provoking indignation back in Britain. His American novels, most notably *A Single Man*, both reflected his newfound spiritual interests and blazed a trail for the gay liberation movement.

In this new biography, Jake Poller takes a holistic approach to Isherwood, exploring the development of his innovative autofiction and unpacking the Vedanta philosophy that informed his later work. He provides an incisive account of an iconic figure.

Jake Poller teaches in the English department at Queen Mary University of London. His books include *Aldous Huxley* (Reaktion, 2021).

With 21 illustrations

Reaktion Books Ltd
www.reaktionbooks.co.uk

ISBN 978-1-83639-009-1

9 781836 390091